AMERICAN
HERITAGE

February 1964 · Volume XV, Number 2

ON HISTORY

By JOHN F. KENNEDY

President Kennedy, who now so prematurely and tragically belongs to history, not only made history himself but wrote it with depth and eloquence. His heightened perceptions of it pervaded his actions and his public papers. Astonishingly in so busy a man, he could even find time in the White House to keep up his intellectual interests, to read good books, and to write prefaces and occasional pieces. Last year he was kind enough, at our request, to furnish an introduction to a sixteen-volume set of books that we created, **The American Heritage New Illustrated History of the United States,** *recently published by the Dell Publishing Company. It would have been easy enough to muster a few bland platitudes, and dash them off, as so many people do in such circumstances, but that was not his way. Instead he sent us this moving essay. It compresses into brief compass much of the philosophy that animates the historical profession. We are proud to reprint it here.* —O. J.

There is little that is more important for an American citizen to know than the history and traditions of his country. Without such knowledge, he stands uncertain and defenseless before the world, knowing neither where he has come from nor where he is going. With such knowledge, he is no longer alone but draws a strength far greater than his own from the cumulative experience of the past and a cumulative vision of the future.

Knowledge of our history is, first of all, a pleasure for its own sake. The American past is a record of stirring achievement in the face of stubborn difficulty. It is a record filled with figures larger than life, with high drama and hard decision, with valor and with tragedy, with incidents both poignant and picturesque, and with the excitement and hope involved in the conquest of a wilderness and the settlement of a continent. For the true historian—and for the true student of history—history is an end in itself. It fulfills a deep human need for understanding, and the satisfaction it provides requires no further justification.

Yet, though no further justification is required for the study of history, it would not be correct to say that history serves no further use than the satisfaction of the historian. History, after all, is the memory of a nation. Just as memory enables the individual to learn, to choose goals and stick to them, to avoid making the same mistake twice—in short, to grow—so history is the means by which a nation establishes its sense of identity and purpose. The future arises out of the past, and a country's history is a statement of the values and hopes which, having forged what has gone before, will now forecast what is to come.

As a means of knowledge, history becomes a means of judgment. It offers an understanding of both the variety and unity of a nation whose motto is *E Pluribus Unum*—out of many, one. It reminds us of the diverse abundance of our people, coming from all races and all parts of the world, of our fields and mountain ranges, deserts and great rivers, our green farmlands and the thousand voices of our cities. No revolution in communication or transportation can destroy the fact that this continent is, as Walt Whitman said, "a nation of nations." Yet it also reminds us that, in spite of the diversity of ethnic origin, of geographic locale, of occupation, of social status, of religious creed, of political commitment, Americans are united by an ancient and encompassing faith in progress, justice, and freedom.

Our history thus tests our policy: Our past judges our present. Of all the disciplines, the study of the folly and achievements of man is best calculated to foster the critical sense of what is permanent and meaningful amid the mass of superficial and transient questions which make up the day-to-day clamor. The history of our nation tells us that every action taken *against* the freedoms of conscience and expression, *against* equality before the law and equality of opportunity, *against* the ordinary men and women of the country is an action taken *against* the American tradition. And it tells us that every action taken *for* a larger freedom and a more equal and spacious society is one more step toward realization of what Herbert Croly once called "the promise of American life."

A knowledge of history is more than a means of judgment: It is also a means of sympathy—a means of relating our own experience with the experience of other peoples and lands struggling for national fulfillment. We may sometimes forget, for example, that the United States began as an underdeveloped nation which seized its independence by carrying out a successful revolution against a colonial empire. We may forget that, in the first years of the new republic, George Washington laid down the principle of no "permanent alliances" and enjoined the United States to a course of neutralism in the face of the great-power conflicts then dividing the civilized world. We may forget that, in the first stages of our economic development, our national growth was stimulated to a considerable degree by "foreign aid"—that is, investment from abroad—and by public investment and direction on the part of our state and local as well as our national government. We may forget that our own process of economic change was often accompanied by the issue of wildcat paper money, by the repudiation of bonds, by disorder, fraud, and violence. If we recall the facts of our own past, we may better understand the problems and predicaments of contemporary "new nations" laboring for national development in circumstances far less favorable than our own—and we will, in consequence, become less liable to the self-righteousness which is both unworthy of our own traditions and a bane of international relations.

A knowledge of history is, in addition, a means of strength. "In times of change and danger," John Dos Passos wrote just before World War II, "when there is a quicksand of fear under men's reasoning, a sense of continuity with generations gone before can stretch like a life line across the scary present." Dos Passos called his book *The Ground We Stand On*—and the title concisely defines the role of the past in preparing us for the crisis of the present and the challenge of the future. When Americans fight for individual liberty, they have Thomas Jefferson and James Madison beside them; when they strive for social justice, they strive alongside Andrew Jackson and Franklin Roosevelt; when they work for peace and a world community, they work with Woodrow Wilson; when they fight and die in wars to make men free, they fight and die with Abraham Lincoln. Historic continuity with the past, as Justice Oliver Wendell Holmes said, "is not a duty; it is only a necessity."

A knowledge of history is, above all, a means of responsibility—of responsibility to the past and of responsibility to the future . . . of responsibility to those who came before us and struggled and sacrificed to pass on to us our precious inheritance of freedom . . . and of responsibility to those who will come after us and to whom we must pass on that inheritance with what new strength and substance it is within our power to add. "Fellow citizens," Abraham Lincoln said, "we cannot escape history. . . . The fiery trial through which we pass will light us down, in honor or dishonor, to the latest generation." American history is not something dead and over. It is always alive, always growing, always unfinished—and every American today has his own contribution to make to the great fabric of tradition and hope which binds all Americans, dead and living and yet to be born, in a common faith and a common destiny.

4

AMERICAN HERITAGE

The Magazine of History

PUBLISHER
James Parton
EDITORIAL DIRECTOR
Joseph J. Thorndike, Jr.
SENIOR EDITOR
Bruce Catton

EDITOR
Oliver Jensen
MANAGING EDITOR
Robert L. Reynolds
ASSOCIATE EDITORS
Robert Cowley
E. M. Halliday
Richard M. Ketchum
Joan Paterson Mills
ASSISTANT EDITORS
Lyndall Dyer
Stephen W. Sears
CONTRIBUTING EDITOR
Barbara Klaw
LIBRARIAN
Caroline Backlund
COPY EDITOR
Beverly Hill
ASSISTANT: Suzanne Smith

SENIOR ART DIRECTOR
Irwin Glusker

ART DIRECTOR
Murray Belsky
STAFF PHOTOGRAPHER: Herbert Loebel

ADVISORY BOARD
Allan Nevins, *Chairman*

Carl Carmer   Louis C. Jones
Gerald Carson   Alvin M. Josephy, Jr.
Marshall B. Davidson Harry Shaw Newman
John A. Garraty   Howard H. Peckham
Eric F. Goldman   Francis S. Ronalds
          S. K. Stevens

AMERICAN HERITAGE is published every two months by American Heritage Publishing Co., Inc., 551 Fifth Avenue, New York 17, N.Y. Correspondence about subscriptions should be addressed to: American Heritage Subscription Office, 383 West Center Street, Marion, Ohio. Single Copies: $3.95. Annual Subscriptions: $15.00 in U.S. & Canada; $16.00 elsewhere.

An annual Index of AMERICAN HERITAGE is published every February, priced at $1.00. A Cumulative Index of Volumes VI–X is available at $3.00.

AMERICAN HERITAGE will consider but assumes no responsibility for unsolicited material. Title registered U.S. Patent Office. Second class postage paid at New York, N.Y., and at additional mailing offices.

Sponsored by

American Association for State & Local History · Society of American Historians

CONTENTS *February, 1964 · Volume XV, Number 2*

COVER: This stirring view of Philadelphia volunteers assembling during the War of 1812 is the work of Paul Svinin, a young Russian aristocrat who was secretary to Czar Alexander's consul general in America. The mounted figures in the background are members of the City Troop (more properly, the First Troop, Philadelphia City Cavalry); founded before the Revolution, the Troop is still in existence today, though its gatherings are more social or ceremonial than martial. An article about the friendly and perceptive Russian diplomat—and a portfolio of scenes he drew in Philadelphia and elsewhere in the young republic during his twenty-two months here—begins on page 49. All the water colors are in the Metropolitan Museum of Art. *Back Cover:* The famous cowboy artist Charles M. Russell made this foot-high comic figurine, now owned by the Kennedy Galleries, as a New Year's present for a friend.

He had a reputation as a bold, resourceful commander. Yet in battle after battle he had George Washington beaten—and failed to pursue the advantage. Was "Sir Billy" all glitter and no gold? Or was he actually in sympathy with the rebellion?

By THOMAS J. FLEMING

The ENIGMA of GENERAL HOWE

Bloody Bunker Hill was Howe's first Revolutionary battle.

"Had Sir William Howe fortified the Hills round Boston, he could not have been disgracefully driven from it: had he pursued his Victory at Long Island, he had ended the Rebellion: Had he landed above the lines at New York, not a Man could have escaped him: Had he fought the Americans at the Brunx, he was sure of Victory: had he cooperated with the N. Army, he had saved it, or had he gone to Philadelphia by land, he had ruined Mr. Washington and his Forces: But as he did none of these things, had he gone to ye D———l before he was sent to America, it had been a saving of infamy to himself and of indelible dishonour to this country."

These searing words, from a secret memorandum found in the British Headquarters papers, were written by Sir Henry Clinton, the man who succeeded Sir William Howe as Commander in Chief of the British army in North America. They sum up one view of this strange general into whose hands George III first confided the power to extinguish the rebellion of his North American colonies. But it is by no means the only view. When Howe was relieved as Commander in Chief in 1778, we have John André's testimony that "the most gallant of our officers, and those whom I least suspected of giving such instances of their affection, shed tears while they bade him farewell."

To Loyalist Joseph Galloway, on the other hand, Howe was nothing but a colossal blunderer. "Blunder upon blunder is incessantly rising in its view," he wrote in a pamphlet after Howe resigned, "and as they rise they increase in magnitude . . . so that their possibility almost exceeds the utmost extent of our belief." Even more sinister was the opinion of another Loyalist, who wrote a letter from New York describing both the General and his brother, Vice Admiral Richard Howe, who at the same time commanded the British fleet in American waters. "The Howes are both antiministerial men," the Loyalist wrote, "and their minds are poisoned by faction: they have endeavoured by every means to spare the Rebellion in order to give it and the Rebels an air of consequence at home."

The British Parliament was as baffled by William Howe as everyone else. After he resigned, a committee investigated his conduct of the war. Howe submitted his vast correspondence with Lord George Germain, Secretary of State for American Colonies, plus a forty-page narrative; numerous other witnesses, including such distinguished generals as Charles Cornwallis, testified, mostly in Howe's favor. But the committee never made a report.

American opinion of Howe is equally confused and confusing. Alexander Hamilton called him that "unintelligible gentleman." Israel Putnam said flatly that Sir William was either "a friend of America or no general." And John Adams wrote to his wife that it was "impossible to discover the designs of an enemy who has no design at all." But Major General Charles Lee, who knew Howe well, hailed him as an "executive soldier in which capacity he is all fire and activity, brave and cool as Julius Caesar."

This much we certainly know: During his two and one half years as British Commander in Chief, William Howe never lost a battle when he was in personal charge of his army. Every time he met Washington in the field, he thrashed him unmercifully. Yet Howe failed to end the rebellion. Again and again, Washington escaped to fight another day. The climax to this strange reversal of the rules of war was Saratoga. While Howe was whipping Washington at Brandywine and Germantown and capturing Philadelphia, the capital of the new United States of America, he was simultaneously turning his back on John Burgoyne and his northern army, to the ultimate disaster of the British cause. Burgoyne's surrender at Saratoga brought France into the war and turned a family quarrel into a world conflict for which England was totally unprepared. Even as he marched his triumphant regiments into the rebel capital, Howe could justly be accused of losing the war.

What went on in Howe's head is a question which historians have been debating ever since. Unfortunately there is very little genuine evidence. The Howe family papers were destroyed by a fire in 1845, and Sir William was not given to writing personal memoranda, in the style of Sir Henry Clinton. He was also a notably taciturn man, so there is even a scarcity of personal statements passed on by third parties. But the evidence we do have tells us a good deal, and most of it puts the Revolution in a light seldom seen in American textbooks.

When William Howe arrived in America in the spring of 1775, he was forty-five years old, a solidly built, six-foot soldier with snapping black eyes and a glittering reputation. In the French and Indian War he had been the daring young colonel who led the "forlorn hope" up the supposedly impregnable Heights of Abraham, to bring on the battle which won Quebec and Canada. Howe had fought with distinction in other actions, too, notably the siege of Havana and the foray against Belle Isle, off the coast of France. Throughout his army career he had been known as a daredevil, a reputation he enhanced, in the intervals between wars, by a passionate fondness for the gambling table.

Long Island: Howe is overcautious, and the quarry flees. After a brilliant flanking maneuver had driven the shaken Americans into redoubts on Brooklyn Heights, Howe abandoned his assault for siege tactics. In darkness Washington got his men back to Manhattan, his one consolation being the delaying action of the Maryland and Delaware troops (above) which had helped his main body survive the initial attack.

The Howe family had a tradition of friendship with America. The oldest brother, Lord George Augustus Howe, had died in the battle for Fort Ticonderoga in 1758 (expiring in Israel Putnam's arms), and the Commonwealth of Massachusetts had erected a monument in his honor in Westminster Abbey. It was to Howe's next oldest brother, Admiral Lord Richard Howe, that Benjamin Franklin turned in a last desperate effort to heal the growing breach between the colonies and the mother country.

The Howes were Whigs, members of an opposition to George III's harsh colonial policy that included Edmund Burke and the violent Charles James Fox, who declared that if he had lived in America, he would have been among the first to take up arms against the Tory-dominated Parliament. William Howe held the family seat in the House of Commons, and in order to placate the pro-American merchants of Nottingham in the election of 1774, he had declared that he would never accept a commission to serve against America. More than a few of his constituents took a dim view of

the way he forgot this campaign promise when George III proffered the job, and they let the General know it. On February 21, 1775, shortly before he sailed for America, Howe gave them a most significant answer.

My going thither was not of my seeking, I was ordered, and could not refuse without incurring the odious name of backwardness to serve my country in distress. So contrary are men's opinions here [in London] to some with you, that instead of the grossest abuse, I have been most highly complimented upon the occasion by those who are even averse to the measures of the administration. Every man's private feelings ought to give way to the service of the public at all times; but particularly when of that delicate nature in which our affairs stand at present . . . One word for America: you are deceived if you suppose there are not many loyal and peaceable subjects in that country. I may safely assert that the insurgents are very few, in comparison of the whole people . . . With respect to the few, who, I am told, desire to separate themselves from the Mother Country, I trust, when they find they are not supported in their frantic ideas by the more moderate, which I have described, they will, from fear of punishment, subside to the laws . . .

Kip's Bay: Howe lands at the wrong place. Less than a month after the Battle of Long Island, Howe made an amphibious landing near where 34th Street now meets the East River. Had he come ashore farther north, he might have sealed off the Americans on Manhattan Island; even as it was, the British barrage so demoralized them that they might have been beaten easily. Instead, Howe dug in on the beachhead.

Almost every line of this letter is important. Howe speaks of "private feelings" which he frankly admits he is suppressing for the sake of public policy. Above all he bases his case on the supposition that he is going to the colonies not to oppress a free people, but to rescue the majority from the tyranny of a few demagogues. He also makes a special point of letting his constituents know that those "averse to the measures of the administration"—by which he meant men like Fox and Burke—have complimented him. Why would Fox —and especially Burke, who was about to make his great plea to the unheeding Parliament for the conciliation of the American colonies—compliment Howe, unless they thought he was going to heal wounds, rather than to make fresh ones?

But when Howe arrived in America on May 25, 1775, the time for conciliation was all but over. British and American blood had been spilled at Lexington and Concord, and the British army was penned inside Boston by an aroused host of New Englanders. On June 16, 1775, they seized a height known as Breed's

Hill, opposite Boston, and the next day General Thomas Gage sent Howe and a picked army of regulars across the harbor to drive the motley collection of patriots off their offensive perch. The Battle of Bunker Hill was Howe's first fight with "the loyal and peaceable subjects" in America. Before his unbelieving eyes, he saw England's best regiments decimated by the entrenched Americans, and only the most frantic efforts on the part of the General and his officers drove the battered redcoats up the hill one last time, to oust the rebels—out of ammunition now—from their fort. Always famed for his daredevil courage, Howe exposed himself fearlessly throughout the furious fight, but he wrote home to his brother that in the midst of the carnage, "There was a moment I never felt before."

What was that moment? Was it the simple possibility of defeat? Howe had experienced that before. At the now-forgotten battle of St. Foy, the year after Wolfe's victory at Quebec, Howe's regiment had lost almost fifty per cent of its men, and the British had had to retreat helter-skelter behind Quebec's walls,

9

where only the arrival of reinforcements rescued them. The moment of Bunker Hill may well have involved something more complex: the horror of seeing men of the same blood slaughtering each other, the realization that he—and the British government—were wildly wrong when they "safely asserted" that "the insurgents are very few." Finally, was there the born gambler's flash of insight that this American war was "wrong" in the most profound sense of the word, and

that in it British generals were never to enjoy that "luck" which most professional soldiers, and especially the daredevils, believe is as important in war as strategic genius? The questions are worth considering.

Not long after Bunker Hill, George III appointed Howe Commander in Chief of the British army in North America as successor to Thomas Gage, who had a reputation for losing battles and for being too "soft" on the rebels. Months of stalemate followed. Howe

10

Saratoga: Howe turns his back on Burgoyne. *In 1777 General John Burgoyne started southward from Canada in an effort to isolate New England by joining up at Albany with Howe driving northward from New York and Barry St. Leger pushing eastward through the Mohawk Valley. Instead, Howe went off to take Philadelphia, the rebel capital, and St. Leger never reached the rendezvous. Partly because of the gallantry of Benedict Arnold—shown above on a white charger at Freeman's Farm near Saratoga—the Americans forced Burgoyne to surrender. At right, the British General Simon Fraser, mortally wounded by a sniper, is carried from the field.*

declared it was impossible to act offensively from Boston with his small army—he had less than 10,000 men —and the government agreed. But the Navy, disastrously neglected during a decade of peace, could not immediately muster enough ships to evacuate Howe's troops from Boston. Meanwhile, in spite of repeated demands from the Whig opposition, the King's ministers did nothing to reverse the drift toward all-out war. Finally, early in 1776, they found a compromise

CONTINUED ON PAGE 96

11

As dawn approached on the morning of May 25, 1863, General William S. Rosecrans, the Union commander in Tennessee, found himself in charge of a prisoner he would soon and gladly be rid of. The man was Clement L. Vallandigham—the most reviled member of that controversial political sect of the American Civil War, the Copperheads. A former United States congressman from Ohio recently defeated for re-election, Vallandigham had achieved notoriety by denouncing Abraham Lincoln as a dictator and by demanding an immediate armistice to end the war, with full restoration of the South's constitutional rights and privileges. His real game, many believed, was to accomplish the permanent separation of the South and the acceptance of its independence by the North.

Vallandigham's views, which he had given unbridled expression in an unending round of orations in the East and West, had roiled countless loyal Unionists. During his membership in the House of Representatives, petitions had poured out of Ohio electoral districts calling for his expulsion from the House as a "traitor and a disgrace to the State." Five months after the outbreak of war, one of Vallandigham's staunchest supporters was writing, "There is no denying the fact now that he is the most unpopular man in the north, and that here in his own district he has but a minority of the people with him."

Just three weeks had passed since the long-gathering storm of condemnation had finally crashed down upon Vallandigham. On May 7, 1863, a military commission had tried him and found him guilty of publicly expressing sentiments calculated to hinder the suppression of the rebellion; he had been sentenced to prison. But President Lincoln had come up with a better idea: he simply ordered the troublesome Vallandigham exiled to the South, behind Confederate battle lines, for the rest of the war.

Now, as he prepared to hand his prisoner over to the Rebels, General Rosecrans provided him the benefit of a polite lecture on loyalty which concluded with the emphatic observation that were Vallandigham not

under heavy guard, Rosecrans' soldiers would tear him to pieces. "That, sir," Vallandigham answered evenly, "is because they are just as prejudiced and ignorant of my character and career as yourself . . ."

"I have a proposition to make," Vallandigham continued. "Draw your soldiers up in a hollow square tomorrow morning, and announce to them that Vallandigham desires to vindicate himself, and I will guarantee that when they have heard me through they will be more willing to tear Lincoln and yourself to pieces than they will Vallandigham." Rosecrans, of course, refused, but the rest of their conversation was amiable enough; when it was time to depart for the Confederate lines, the General laid his hand on Vallandigham's shoulder and said to an aide, "He don't look a bit like a traitor, now does he, Joe?"

History, in whose approving judgment Vallandigham had indestructible faith, has not smiled upon him. The prevailing view is that he was a traitor, or at best only a half-step removed from being one. Yet for all of the severity and assurance with which the verdict has been rendered, history's estimation of Vallandigham is still open to question. Although he stands in no danger of becoming a national hero, several key facts of his career remain shrouded in doubt, and the good that he did, which was not unimportant, has been interred with his bones.

What manner of man was Clement Laird Vallandigham? He was born in New Lisbon, Ohio, on July 29, 1820, the son of a Presbyterian minister of southern extraction. Young Clement's upbringing included a thorough grounding in religion and study at Jefferson College at Canonsburg, Pennsylvania, which at the time had a large southern clientele. Upon returning to Ohio, he practiced law in New Lisbon and subsequently in Dayton and went into politics. A spellbinding champion of the Jeffersonian vision of individual liberty, local autonomy, and agrarian simplicity, he served in the Ohio legislature and, commencing in 1858, in the United States House of Representatives.

Vallandigham's congressional career was largely de-

the north"

By LOUIS W. KOENIG

Peace without victory was the crusade of Clement L. Vallandigham, the volatile extremist spokesman of the antiwar "Copperheads." Too often his deeds had a suspicious odor of treason

"The Constitution as it is, the Union as it was," proclaimed Vallandigham in his demagogic campaign to end the Civil War. The Ohio politician is shown at right in a photograph by Mathew Brady. Above, a cartoon of 1863 shows the Copperheads (they were officially known as Peace Democrats) about to strike at a beleaguered Union; the threat was not wholly empty.

CULVER PICTURES

MESERVE COLLECTION

voted to assailing the abolitionists, whose antislavery preachings, he believed, were impairing the general peace and harmony and threatening the dissolution of the Union. To preserve peace—which was the natural interest of the Midwest with its acute dependence upon unfettered use of the Mississippi—Vallandigham counselled a strict observance of states' rights. "With the domestic policies and institutions of Kentucky, or any other State," he declared, "the people have no more right to intermeddle than with the laws or form of government in Russia. Slavery in the South is to them as polygamy in the Turkish Empire."

But the exhortations of Vallandigham and others in Congress who sincerely advocated peace were all in vain. The states of the Deep South seceded, the Confederacy was established, Fort Sumter was attacked, and the Union disintegrated in the roaring furnace of war.

Vallandigham's position in the new state of affairs was quickly and candidly revealed. He refused to aid the war by word or deed. "I had rather my right arm were plucked from its socket, and cast into eternal burnings," he cried in his theatrical fashion. When a gigantic army appropriation bill went before the House, Vallandigham tried to attach an amendment that would have required the President to appoint commissioners to accompany the army on the march and receive and consider propositions looking toward the suspension of hostilities and the return of the Confederate states to the Union.

By far the most fertile ground for Vallandigham's opposition to the Lincoln administration was the vital issue of freedom and civil liberty. The Constitution's requirements concerning both the fundamental procedures of government and the protection of individual rights were being rapidly and sweepingly subordinated to the exigencies of war. In the ten weeks between the outbreak of hostilities at Fort Sumter and the convening of Congress on July 4, Lincoln expanded the Army and Navy without authorization of Congress; applied unappropriated funds of the Treasury to their support; and levied a blockade without the prior declaration of war by Congress contemplated by the Constitution. Above all, he suspended the writ of habeas corpus in various parts of the country and caused the arrest and military detention of individuals "who were represented to him" as persons engaging in or contemplating "treasonable practices." "Are all the laws *but one* to go unexecuted," asked Lincoln in justifying his extraordinary actions, "and the Government itself to go to pieces lest that one be violated . . . ?"

The Lincoln government, in short, had an authoritarian side, and Vallandigham was its most tireless and articulate critic. He flayed the President for not assem-

CONTINUED ON PAGE 81

14

On August 31, 1864, the Democratic convention meeting at the National Amphitheatre in Chicago (below) nominated for President the popular former commander of the Army of the Potomac, General George B. McClellan. But Vallandigham and others in the Copperhead wing of the party seriously hurt "Little Mac's" chances by forcing into the platform a plank which called the war a failure and demanded an immediate end to hostilities. (During these eventful days, an attempt by Confederate agents in the city to foment an uprising by Copperhead sympathizers fizzled out.) Having nominated a war hero and, with equal enthusiasm, declared for peace, the delegates had created a paradox which their Republican opponents did not hesitate to exploit. The cartoon at right depicts a two-faced McClellan standing on a rickety platform upheld by Jefferson Davis, the pro-southern London Times, Vallandigham, and a fellow Copperhead, Mayor Fernando Wood of New York City.

THE CHICAGO PLATFORM AND CANDIDATE.

One innovation profoundly changed—and prolonged—the culture

George Catlin's portrait of a Crow chief in full regalia typifies the image of the mounted Indian, romantic yet formidable, and suggests his proud sense of utter identification with his horse. The Crows' uncut hair rivalled their horses' tails in splendor.

HOW THE INDIAN GOT THE HORSE

By FRANCIS HAINES

On Thursday, May 24, 1855, Lieutenant Law-rence Kip of the U.S. Army, stationed at Fort Walla Walla in what is now Washington, made this entry in his diary:

This has been an extremely interesting day, as about 2,500 of the Nez Percé tribe have arrived. It was our first speci-men of this Prairie chivalry, and it certainly realized all our conceptions of these wild warriors of the plains. Their coming was announced about 10 o'clock, and going out on the plain to where a flag staff had been erected, we saw them approaching in one long line. They were almost en-tirely naked, gaudily painted and decorated with their wild trappings. Their plumes fluttered about them, while below, skins and trinkets of all kinds of fantastic embellishments flaunted in the sunshine. Trained from early childhood almost to live upon horseback, they sat upon their fine animals as if they were centaurs. Their horses, too, were arrayed in the most glaring finery. They were painted with such colors as formed the greatest contrast; the white being smeared with crimson in fantastic figures, and the dark colors streaked with white clay. Beads and fringes, of gaudy colors were hanging from the bridles, while the plumes of eagle feathers interwoven with the mane and tail, fluttered as the breeze swept over them, and completed their wild and fantastic appearance.

This image of the proud Indian on his splendid horse, both of them splashed with gaudy war paint and adorned with feathered devices, seems to personify the spirit of the old West in those far-off times before the buffalo herds were all slaughtered and barbed wire had enclosed the high plains. Very probably young Lieutenant Kip, like most white people of his day, accepted without question the idea that the Indians had always had horses. They were obviously an in-separable and essential element of Indian culture on the Great Plains; and indeed, the first Anglo-Americans to reach those areas, in the latter part of the eighteenth century, had found the mounted Indians already in full force. Yet in 1855 less than 150 years had passed since the first Nez Percé ever to mount a horse had taken his first daring ride.

The fossil discoveries of the later nineteenth century made it clear that, although prehistoric horses had roamed the western plains in large numbers for a mil-lion years, some odd, selective catastrophe wiped them out, along with camels, perhaps 15,000 years ago. Hence, when the Spanish explorers of the sixteenth century rode their horses into the Southwest, the In-dians gazed with wonder at the strange beasts. The process by which the native tribes adopted the animal, and consequently were able to hold the land against all intruders until the destruction of the buffalo herds starved them into submission, has been the subject of much speculation and dispute.

Until recent years historians and anthropologists accepted rather casually the theory that horses lost from early Spanish expeditions had, by natural in-crease, stocked the western ranges with wild bands that supplied the various Indian tribes with their animals. The favored choice for the supposed source of the breeding stock was either the expedition of Hernando de Soto or that of Francisco Vásquez de Coronado, both of which reached the plains of Texas in 1541–42.

De Soto, after conquering Peru, had returned to Spain, married, and secured the governorship of Cuba, with the privilege of exploring and conquering Florida and the land to the north and west. His quest ended when he died of fever on the shore of the Mississippi River in May, 1542. The remnants of his forces, led by Luis Moscoso, travelled west and south to Texas in a vain attempt to reach Mexico overland. Failing in this, they returned to the Mississippi and built a fleet of seven brigantines on which they embarked with 22 horses, all that were left of their original 243.

As the Spaniards sailed down the river they killed the horses one by one for food, until only five or six of the best were left. These they turned loose in a small, grassy meadow near the mouth of the river. Legend would have it that these horses remembered the plains of Texas and wished to return there. They swam the river, splashed through a hundred miles of swamps and marshes, and finally reached open country with abundant grass. Here, supposedly, they settled down and reproduced at a prodigious rate. Soon their offspring covered the Texas plains and attracted the attention of the local Indians, who knew how to catch and train them from having seen the Spanish ride by on such animals years ago.

Stubborn facts undermine this pretty tale. First, one of the Spaniards in Moscoso's party said later that Indians came out of the bushes and shot the liberated horses full of arrows even before the Spanish boats had passed beyond the next bend. Second, even if they had survived, the route to the west was impassable for horses, which in any case had no way of knowing the direction to take to reach Texas. Third, and finally, these war horses were all stallions. The Spanish rode no other kind to battle. For these reasons it is obvious that de Soto's animals could not have stocked the western plains with horses, wild or tame.

The other candidate, Francisco Coronado, approached Texas from the west. He started from Mexico City, mustered his expedition at Compostela, and marched north to Arizona, then east to New Mexico and on to Texas. In 1541 he approached the Plains with a force estimated at 1,500 people, 1,000 horses, 500 cattle, and 5,000 sheep. He spent more than five months on the Plains, where he lost many horses. Some were gored by buffalo, some fell into a ravine during a buffalo chase. A few might have strayed away without their loss being noted by the chronicler, and it is conceivable that a stallion and a mare might have strayed off together. The muster rolls of the expedition list two mares starting out from Compostela, and there might have been a few more not listed.

Assume, then, that such a pair escaped in northern Texas, adjusted to the range conditions, and produced offspring, all of whom survived. It is mathematically possible that in sixty years or so the resulting herd would number several thousand. They would have ranged the plains for hundreds of miles, leaving their spoor at every water hole. Yet Spanish explorers and buffalo hunters from the later Sante Fe settlements found no wild horses of any kind in this area before 1700. It seems reasonable, then, that any such strays were wiped out by bad water, storms, accidents, and predators such as the wolf and cougar. These hazards to the foals should not be discounted; in 1719 the Paducahs reported that they had not been able to raise any colts, but had to obtain all their horses by barter—and they had owned horses for several years by that time.

Nor could even the most intelligent Indian hope to learn the art of catching, breaking, and training wild horses just from watching the Spanish ride by on tame ones. For a primitive people to learn such a complex pattern in a short space of time, they must have skilled horsemen for teachers and gentle, well-trained horses to handle. Even under these conditions such learning is sometimes difficult.

For example, according to Flathead tradition, their tribe secured a gentle horse in western Montana around 1700, and some of them attempted to ride it. One man would lead the horse slowly along while the rider attempted to balance himself with the aid of two long sticks, one in each hand, reaching to the ground like crutches. When one of the young men finally managed to ride unaided at a trot, he was the hero of the whole band.

The simplest and most effective way for the Indians of the Southwest to learn how to break, train, and care for horses was for them to work for the Spaniards. Such an opportunity was forced on the Pueblo Indians of New Mexico in the seventeenth century.

In 1595 Philip II of Spain commissioned Juan de Oñate, a wealthy citizen of Zacatecas, to conquer and settle the upper valley of the Rio Grande del Norte, where the Pueblo Indians lived in their farming villages. Early in the spring of 1598 Oñate led forth his caravan of soldiers and settlers, with their families and slaves, both Indian and Negro. Franciscan friars accompanied the caravan to care for the spiritual needs of the settlers and to convert the heathen.

They travelled north across Chihuahua and through the great gap in the mountains, El Paso del Norte. There they crossed the Rio Grande and swung east and north to avoid the river canyon. Finally they reached the upper valley with its Indian settlements and took possession of all the land, forcing the Pueblos to work as serfs in the fields they had once owned.

The Spanish brought herds of sheep, cattle, and horses to pasture on the desert ranges. Herding these animals was an endless task, for there were no fences of any kind on the pasture lands and no adequate material for building them until the invention of barbed wire some two and a half centuries later. Even the cultivated fields in the alluvial soil along the valley floor went unfenced from lack of material. Hence herdsmen were needed day and night to keep the flocks and herds from straying, to protect the animals from predators, and to keep them out of the growing crops.

Indian herdsmen proved adept at managing the sheep and goats, moving them to fresh pastures and holding them away from the fields. This they could do

TEXT CONTINUED ON PAGE 78
ILLUSTRATIONS CONTINUED ON FOLLOWING PAGES

Indian horse herds were replenished by capture as well as by trade. George Catlin's Comanche brave, above, has lassoed and hobbled a wild horse, and now subdues him with a rope tied around the lower jaw. The warriors in Carl Wimar's painting, below, are leading the mount of a presumably dead U.S. Army officer back to their camp.

Four aspects of the great change wrought in the life of the Indian by his adoption of the horse are vividly depicted on these two pages. The Swiss artist Carl Bodmer, on his long trip with Prince Maximilian in 1833 (see the Bodmer portfolio in the April, 1963, AMERICAN HERITAGE), caught some Sioux in their favorite diversion of horse racing, near Fort Pierre, South Dakota (above). Left, Charles M. Russell's The Horse of the Hunter *freezes an instant of critical action during an Indian buffalo hunt: the bull has been wounded, and the hunter is notching another arrow for the final coup. The horse is a pinto, favored by many Plains Indians for its natural decorations. Swooping in at full gallop to pick up a fallen comrade under fire was one of the most impressive feats of Indian horsemanship in warfare. Frederic Remington's painting, below, dramatizes such an incident. Opposite: Nomadic by long custom, the Plains Indians became more so after the arrival of the horse. The animal's tremendous capacity for transport, even without wheels. is seen in William Cary's oil,* Indian Migration.

Mason & Dixon: their Line and its Legend

By A. HUGHLETT MASON *and* WILLIAM F. SWINDLER

Lines on maps may be drawn by engineers, but they are interpreted by political events. Seldom has history recorded an amicable and abiding acceptance of such demarcations when they involve restless dynastic movements, whether the example be Pope Alexander VI's division of the New World in 1493 between Spain and Portugal, or the twentieth century's unhappy establishment of the border between East and West Berlin after World War II. The surveyor's work becomes a symbol, and his name may become a catch phrase for a congeries of political and social issues of which he never dreamed.

The prime illustration of such an event in the United States is the line laid out for a total of about 332 miles by two English astronomer-surveyors between 1763 and 1767, to settle a dispute between the Penns and the Baltimores. For more than eighty years these powerful proprietaries had contended over the precise location of their common border. When they finally settled upon these two scientists to direct an impersonal, mathematically dependable survey, they set the stage for an engineering feat of impressive dimensions for that time.

But Charles Mason and Jeremiah Dixon were destined to be remembered for their substantial engineering and scientific accomplishments only in the annals of specialists. Mason, among other things, later completed a catalogue of 387 stars, which, when incorpo-

rated into a nautical almanac published in 1787, became the standard authority on the subject for a number of years. Dixon, a county surveyor and amateur astronomer, was considered sufficiently adept in his field to be elected to the Royal Society. He took part in several overseas scientific expeditions for the Society.

For considerably more than a century, however, what the average American has understood by the Mason-Dixon survey has been a figurative division between two frames of reference in national life. Just as the South—and, for that matter, the North—tended to become a state of mind, so the Mason-Dixon Line has come to be viewed only incidentally as a real border and more as a line of transition between these two states of mind. In the national psychology it is thought of as a jagged extension of the border between Pennsylvania and Maryland to some vaguely defined point on the Missouri-Kansas border.

Just when this popular concept first took shape is not easy to say. Obviously, as sectional consciousness in the matter of slavery increased in the first half of the nineteenth century, the fact that Maryland, the most northerly slave state, was divided from Pennsylvania's free soil by the Mason-Dixon survey impressed itself upon the public mind. The Ohio River, as the border between the southern state of Kentucky and the Northwest Territory, where slavery was prohibited, was a natural landmark extending the symbolism

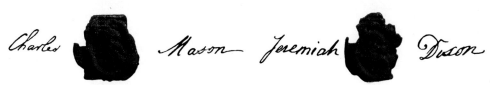

No portraits of either Mason or Dixon are known to exist: their seals and signatures on the original survey contract are shown above. Opposite: a typical Mason-Dixon "crownstone" marker, placed every fifth mile along the line—this one near Rising Sun, Maryland. Though eroded by time, the arms of the Penns are still visible on this northern side; the southern bears Lord Baltimore's.

23

*Below: A map printed in 1732 by Benjamin Franklin anticipated the approximate location of the Mason-Dixon Line. Cape Henlopen, marker for the southern border of the "Three Lower County's"—then part of Pennsylvania, now the state of Delaware—appears twenty miles too far south, near Fenwick Island. But the British Court of Chancery nevertheless accepted that location. **Above and opposite:** A detail from Mason and Dixon's own map shows most of their actual line. As Delaware's lower boundary—from A (extreme lower right) on Fenwick Island to B at Delaware's southwestern corner (five miles west of present-day Delmar, Maryland)—Mason and Dixon accepted the line laid out by earlier surveyors in obedience to the court's fiat. From B they drew their line approximately eighty-two miles northward to the northeastern corner of Maryland—point D here—some eight miles northeast of modern Elkton. Thence they worked 233 miles westward, to Dunkard Creek and the Monongahela (beyond the scope of this map), some twenty miles from Pennsylvania's southwestern tip. In time, "the Mason-Dixon line" meant only this east-west segment plus an imaginary westward extension, and thus a line between slave states and free.*

of the Mason-Dixon Line, the western terminus of which lay close to that great waterway to the West. Finally, the Missouri Compromise, fixing the northern limit of slave territory at latitude 36 degrees 30 minutes north, westward from the Ohio's juncture with the Mississippi, completed the popular image.

The issues which thus developed in the nineteenth century around Mason and Dixon's survey, and made their names a household phrase, have largely obscured the significant political and scientific results of the original project. That project—a border settlement of the eighteenth century—in turn traced its beginnings to issues which arose in the seventeenth century, and even earlier. The problem really started with England's belated decision to launch her own colonizing efforts in the New World, where Spain and Portugal had long preceded her and where she now found the Netherlands, Sweden, and France in close competition.

Sir Walter Raleigh made the first colonization attempt at Roanoke Island in 1585. After failure of this effort the Virginia Companies of London and Plymouth were chartered, and founded the first two permanent English settlements—at Jamestown in 1607, and at Plymouth in 1620. Unfortunately, James I fixed the northernmost limit of the London Company at latitude 41 degrees north and the southernmost limit of the Plymouth Company at 38 degrees north—an overlap that included more than half of what is now Pennsylvania and New Jersey, and all of Maryland. Within this overlapping area, however, neither company was to settle within 100 miles of the other. This arrangement did, in fact, avoid most arguments between the first and second English colonies; but it multiplied the difficulties for those who came after and settled in between.

One of these was George Calvert, the first Lord Baltimore, whose Maryland charter was granted in 1632. In the course of the next fifty years his heirs were able, in various ways, to overcome claims made by the Dutch, the Virginians, and the Swedes. But the real trouble began only after Charles II's grant of Pennsylvania to William Penn in 1681, and a subsequent grant to Penn by James, Duke of York, of land extending south as far as Chesapeake Bay.

Territorial assignments in seventeenth-century charters were vague, and the technical capacity for accu-

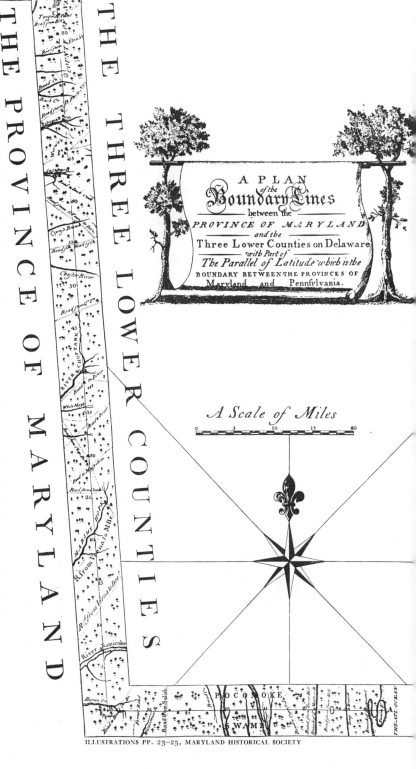

rate fixing of boundaries in the unsettled wilderness was extremely limited. Local surveyors had no particular difficulty in laying out sites for towns and individual plantations. There was a political as well as a surveying problem involved, however, in determining the point described in the Maryland charter as its northern boundary—"that Part of the Bay of Delaware on the North, which lieth under the Fortieth Degree of North Latitude, where New England is terminated."

The fortieth parallel would have put Maryland's northern border somewhere within the present city of Philadelphia. When Penn's grant was made in 1681, Charles Calvert, third Lord Baltimore, insisted that his own prior charter should be interpreted literally. Not so, said Penn's party; the original intent of the Maryland charter was to put the border "under" the fortieth parallel—how far "under" being the point at issue. The vicinity of the fortieth parallel was not unacceptable for the main boundary line, but at its eastern end a vital problem arose. A few miles up or down the Delaware estuary could insure or deprive Pennsylvania of a harbor of enormous commercial potential. In addition, there was the question of which colony was entitled to collect taxes from the settlers within the disputed zone. Bitterly but steadily over the years, the Calverts retreated or were pushed southward from their charter position, particularly in the region of Delaware Bay.

Three times—in 1685, 1732, and 1750—the boundary controversy was adjudicated in England by agencies of the Crown. The upshot was that, by 1760, the Penns' proprietary was held to include roughly half of the northern part of the Delmarva Peninsula, separating Chesapeake Bay from Delaware Bay. It was to include, that is, the area now forming the state of Delaware, but at that time known as the "lower counties" of the Penn domain, or simply as "the counties of Delaware."

Determination of their exact boundaries, however, was a prickly matter. The British Court of Chancery had ruled that the Delaware southern border should be a transpeninsular line extending westward from Cape Henlopen—as that point was indicated on contemporary maps. It turned out that the maps showed the Cape too far south by as much as twenty-two miles; but the Court was stubborn, and the transpeninsular line separating the Penns from the Calverts was drawn

ENOCH PRATT FREE LIBRARY, BALTIMORE

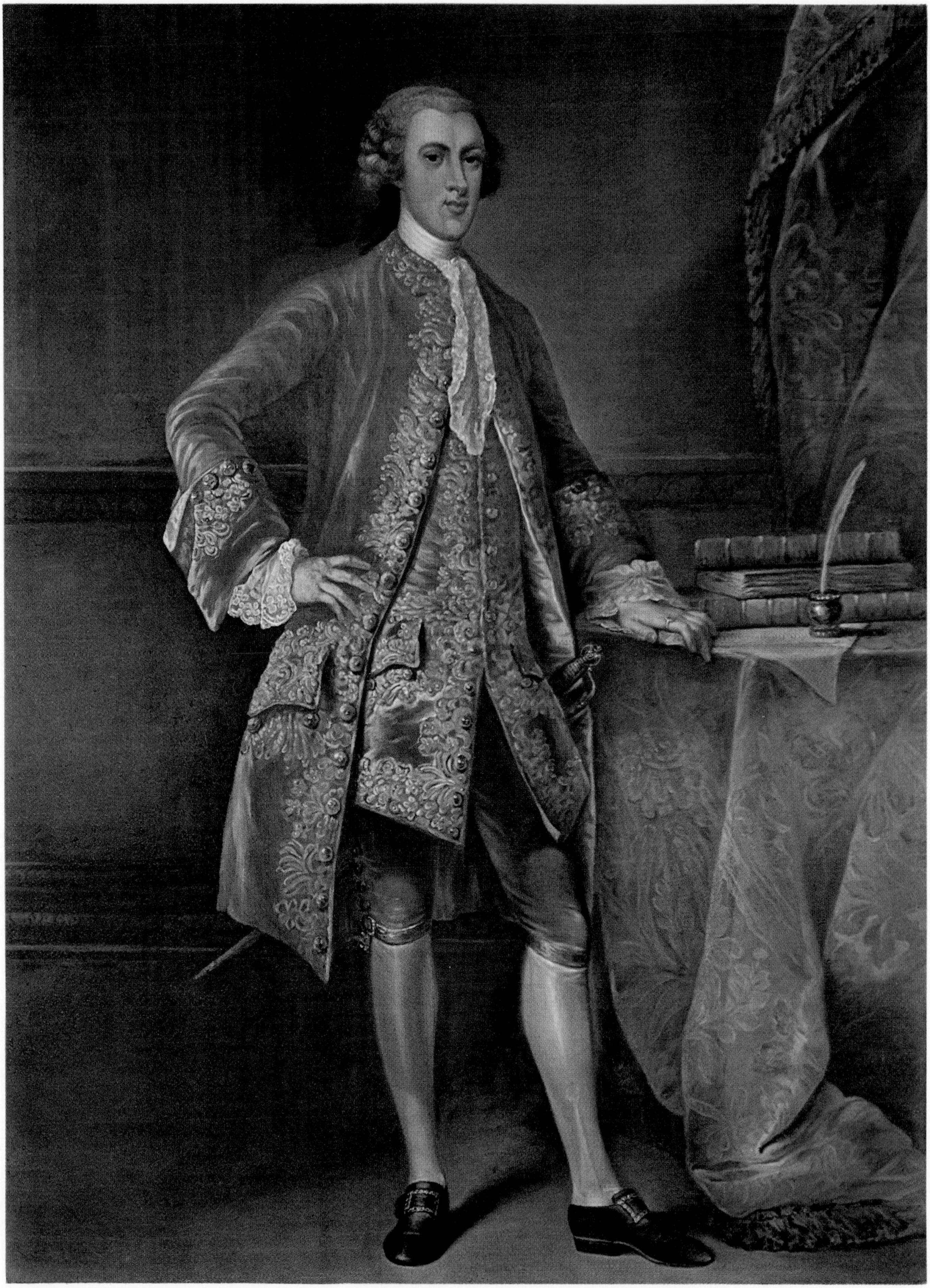

accordingly, to the detriment of the Calverts. The northern boundary of the Delaware counties—which had acquired a form of home rule while remaining within the Penn proprietary—was to be determined by the arc of a circle twelve miles in radius, with its center at New Castle Court House (now New Castle, Delaware).

But the final step—determining the Delaware western border—required the connecting of the midpoint on the transpeninsular line with a tangent point on the arc. The nice astronomical and mathematical steps needed to connect these points proved too much for the colonial commissioners charged with the survey. In 1761, after several months of clearing a line through the wilderness, Thomas Penn's commissioners were compelled to advise him that there had been some basic astronomical miscalculations and "the business set back almost as far as ever." The trouble started, said the commissioners, with a survey telescope that had gone awry; after that everything went wrong.

The telescope "being extended and fixed on a strip of wood . . . after being exposed to a Shower of Rain they perceived the Strip had warped & the Glass did not represent Objects precisely in the places they possessed." Apparently the Penns, accustomed to the considerable scientific sophistication of mid-eighteenth-century England, could not at first believe that the colonials were incapable of handling the problem. A letter from Dr. John Robertson, master of the Royal Naval Academy at Portsmouth, however, assured them of its difficulty and of the need for competent instruments competently used. Added to this was the prospect that erroneous surveys could run into money; as one Pennsylvania commissioner wrote Thomas Penn in 1763, if local scientists surveyed the border, "and if afterwards on Examination of the Work by Mathematicians in England it should be pronounc'd wrong, can Lord Baltimore take advantage of this, set it aside and procure an order to do it over again?"

The obvious solution was "to send over from England some able Mathematicians with a proper set of Mathematical instruments." These persons, in addition to their scientific competence, were to be "of Great Integrity and totally unbiassed and unprejudiced on either side of the question." Eighty years of argument had crystallized the Penns' and Calverts' mutual distrust of each other. Apparently the nomination of the qualified "mathematicians" was solicited from the Astronomer Royal, Charles Bradley, director of the Greenwich Observatory, and his successor, Nathaniel Bliss.

The Astronomer Royal, it happily developed, had the men and the instruments for the job. Charles Mason had been assistant observer at Greenwich from 1756 to 1760, during which time he had worked closely with Bradley on a monumental catalogue of positions of the moon, and on the designing of improved instruments for astronomical observations. And Jeremiah Dixon had early shown enough mathematical precocity to bring him to the attention of John Bird, the creator of many astronomical instruments at Greenwich and a member of the Royal Society. Dixon was described to Penn as a competent surveyor from Durham County, England.

In 1761, England and several leading continental powers had joined in an international scientific project—securing data from more than a hundred points in Europe, Africa, and the Far East during the transit of Venus across the face of the sun, in order to determine more precisely the mean distance between earth and sun. Mason and Dixon drew an assignment to proceed to the island of Sumatra and make observations. A French man-of-war interfered with their sailing schedule, however, and they were able to get only as far as the Cape of Good Hope by the date of the transit. Even so, their observations from that point were praised more than a century later by a scientist at the United States Naval Observatory as being among the most accurate of the whole project.

When in 1762 the two men returned to England by way of the island of St. Helena, they brought information about two instruments that were to figure substantially in their coming assignment in the New World. One was an astronomical clock, made for the Royal Society to aid in determining the ellipticity of the earth. It was this same clock which was later to be shipped to Mason and Dixon to make the New World's first accurate determination of longitude by means of the eclipses of the satellites of Jupiter.

Perhaps more important was the zenith sector which had been used at St. Helena by Mason's mentor, the astronomer Nevil Maskelyne. This instrument, a graduated arc of a vertical circle used in conjunction with a telescope and plumb line, Maskelyne found to have a serious flaw, owing to the manner in which the plumb line was suspended. As a consequence of his findings, the Royal Society at once set to work to construct a corrected sector, and this new instrument was brought by Mason and Dixon when they came to America. It was thus that Thomas Penn could write with confidence to the Reverend Richard Peters, former secretary of the colony, that the right men and the right equipment had at length been found. Messrs. Mason

Frederick Calvert, Sixth Lord Baltimore, whose elegant portrait by Johann Ludwig Tietz appears on the opposite page, authorized the Mason-Dixon survey for his Maryland province, which he never visited.

27

and Dixon, he wrote, would bring with them "the fine Sector, two Transit Instruments, and two reflecting Telescopes, fit to look at the Posts in the Line for ten or twelve miles."

The Penns and Frederick, the sixth Lord Baltimore, having agreed on Mason and Dixon as the realm's best-qualified surveyors, a contract was drawn up on July 20, 1763, stipulating their responsibilities and compensation, the latter to be ten shillings, six pence a day until their arrival in America, and one pound one shilling daily for the period of the survey. The expenses of the project were to be shared equally by the proprietors, and the English scientists were to file identical reports of their findings with the commissioners from each colony. Mason and Dixon were to come to America as soon as possible.

In the course of the protracted dispute over their border, the proprietors had finally agreed that the boundary line between Maryland and Pennsylvania proper should be run east and west along a latitude circle fifteen miles south of the southernmost limit of the city of Philadelphia. The first task for Mason and Dixon on arriving in the colonies was therefore to accurately fix this starting point. The men reached Philadelphia November 15, 1763, unpacked their instruments, and began construction of a small building to serve as their first observatory. By the first of December the "gentlemen commissioners" from Maryland arrived, and in company with those from Pennsylvania, they inspected and confirmed the spot which marked the southernmost limit of the city. After some sixty observations of stars selected from Bradley's *Catalogue*, made over a period of three weeks, Mason and Dixon determined that this spot was at latitude 39 degrees 56 minutes 29.1 seconds north—a finding which later observations showed to be in error only by 2.5 seconds.

Moving westward along this line of latitude to the farm of John Harlan on the Brandywine, "the Telescope &c of the Sector . . . carry'd on the Springs (with feather beds under it) of a Single Horse Chair," the surveyors made further observations from a point where they could run a direct line fifteen miles south —to "a plantation belonging to Mr. Alexander Bryan," the precise spot being in the middle of the front of Mr. Bryan's house. This finding was duly accepted by the two commissions, and the way finally opened for an official determination of the boundary between Pennsylvania and Maryland.

It was long overdue; Mason noted in his journal that the former sheriff of Lancaster had described to him an incident in which a "Mr. Crisep," living on the Susquehanna in territory he maintained was in Maryland, had been set upon by fifty men from Pennsylvania who burned his house and shot one of the besieged party as they ran out. "Mr. Crisep" appears to have been Colonel Thomas Cresap, whose house indeed was burned in 1736—in retaliation, it was alleged, for numerous acts of violence which Cresap's "border ruffians" had precipitated. (The Colonel, incidentally, survived the attack reported to Mason and lived to earn laurels as a patriot in both the French and Indian War and the Revolution.) There were frequent occasions when the border claims of both proprietaries had flared into armed combat.

Mason took a keen interest in all his New World surroundings, both scientific and nonscientific. Once when winter weather suspended surveying, he and his colleague went to New York for a couple of weeks to enjoy the activities of that colonial community. En route they stopped at "Prince Town in the Jersies" and Mason admired "the most elegant built Colledge I've seen in America." On another occasion, when the survey was getting under way, Mason took a short side trip to see a large cave, describing the church-like atmosphere in a lugubrious vein:

On the side walls were drawn by the Pencil of time, with the tears of ye Rocks: the imitation of organ, pillar, collumns and monuments of a Temple; which, with the glinting, faint light, makes the whole an awful, solemn appearance, Striking its Visitors with a strong and melancholy reflection: That, such is the abodes of the Dead; Thy inevitable doom, O Stranger, soon to be numbered as one of Them.

The business at hand, however, occupied most of the scientists' attention. On the Harlan farm, where they set up a more or less permanent headquarters, they erected a crude monument, known by the unindoctrinated for many years after as the "stargazers' stone," and spent much of the snowbound winter making observations.

The Penns and Lord Baltimore had been unduly optimistic as to the period required for the survey, and the deadline had to be extended several times. Weather, transportation, the cumbersome procedure of meeting periodically with the commissioners to make progress reports, and, in the late stages of the project, the threat of Indian interference—all interposed delays. On the whole, however, the parties on both sides were quite satisfied with the work of Mason and Dixon. True, in April of 1764 Governor Horatio Sharpe of Maryland received a letter from Cecilius Calvert, secretary of the colony, alleging that the Penns had offered the Englishmen a contract for the surveying of Pennsylvania's northern border as a *douceur* if the southern border survey treated the Quaker colony right. But on finding that Mason and Dixon had located their original point, fifteen miles south of Philadelphia, a quarter of a mile farther north than previous surveys had indicated, the Calverts' suspicions were quieted.

Before actually surveying the line for the northern boundary of Maryland (39 degrees 43 minutes 17.6 seconds), Mason and Dixon proceeded to establish the Maryland-Delaware boundary. On June 25, 1764, they arrived at the southwest corner of Delaware as established by the colonial surveyors—a point midway on the transpeninsular line running west from where Cape Henlopen was indicated on the early maps. From this point Mason and Dixon ran the tangent line to the New Castle "twelve mile arc." On September 25 they reported that this line, as finally run, lacked only two feet, two inches of tangency to the twelve-mile circle; and as the length of the line was over eighty-two miles, it was accepted by the commissioners.* The scientists stored their instruments for the winter, and the party disbanded to await more favorable weather. On April 4, 1765, Mason and Dixon returned to the Bryan plantation, fifteen miles south of the latitude of Philadelphia, where they set up the zero milestone for the survey of the main segment of their line, the Maryland-Pennsylvania boundary. There they placed a reference marker which in their notes they frequently described as the "Post mark'd West."

In the running of the border Mason and Dixon, using astronomical observation and the laws of spherical geometry, checked their geographical positions every eleven and a half miles—more precisely, every ten minutes of great circle. Deviations were then corrected at each mile point. These points, temporarily marked by posts, were on the true parallel of latitude and

* This survey, when completed, included a 1.466-mile arc of the twelve-mile circle itself, plus a 3.574-mile "North Line" connecting the arc with the northeast corner of Maryland.

represented the boundary between Maryland and Pennsylvania.

To facilitate sighting and marking, the surveyors employed axemen to clear a rough corridor (or "Visto," as they called it) "8 or 9 yards wide" along the points of their periodic observations and measurements. Horizontal measurements were taken with a Gunter's chain of sixty-six links on level ground, and with a triangular-shaped surveyor's "level" on the slopes. By this procedure of making horizontal measurements controlled by astronomical observations they continued westward, until ultimately, on October 9, 1767, they reached a point about 233 miles from the "Post mark'd West," beyond which the Indian tribes refused to permit further work.

The survey was consistently meticulous. "To prove that the Chain Carriers had made no error," Mason wrote in his journal at one point, "I took a Man with me, a few days after, and measured it myself; and made it within a link of the same." After the first twenty-five miles the party (about a dozen persons) retraced their steps and checked their work. By June, 1765, they were again moving westward, crossing the Susquehanna at Peach Bottom, Pennsylvania, and continuing to the summit of the Blue Ridge mountains, which they reached in late October. Here Mason and Dixon suspended the survey for the season, left their instruments "not in the least damaged to our knowledge" with Captain Evan Shelby, a well-known frontiersman, and spent the next few weeks checking their distance measurements as they returned eastward.

The winter months of January and February, 1766, were spent sightseeing in adjacent colonies, including a trip to Williamsburg, "the Metropolis of Virginia,"

CONTINUED ON PAGE 93

Acting for Pennsylvania in the border negotiations were the sons of William Penn. Richard Penn (far right), like Lord Baltimore, never saw the disputed territory; Thomas (right) was in America from 1731 to 1742.

29

THE GREAT WHITE FLEET

By FRANK UHLIG, JR.

In a line three miles long, the battleships of the Great White Fleet thread their way through the perilous Strait of Magellan.

After the Civil War, American sea power became a pitiful joke. Then an aroused nation set out to build a first-class, modern navy, and in 1907 proudly sent it off around the world

The S.S. *Virginius* of New York, Captain Charles Fry, darted up from the Jamaica coast, bound for Cuba, which lay blue in the distance. It was November, 1873. As the ship crossed the brilliant Caribbean, the Spanish gunboat *Tornado* took chase and closed quickly. When the Spaniards boarded, they found the *Virginius* stacked high with arms for Cuba's rebels, then engaged in another of their apparently endless insurrections against the mother country.

The captured ship was taken to Santiago, on Cuba's southern shore. Forty-three of the passengers and crew were bound, lined up against a wall, and shot. The rest were saved only by the arrival of H.M.S. *Niobe*, whose captain insisted that the Spanish governor "stop that filthy slaughter." For a time, war between the United States and Spain seemed unavoidable. President Grant ordered the fleet mobilized at Key West.

A marvelous collection of naval museum pieces gathered there. Eleven old wooden steam frigates and steam sloops, their decks lined with muzzle-loading smoothbores, their masts laden with canvas, made up the cruising force. Five iron monitors, hastily recommissioned, were towed down from the James and the Delaware, where they had been rusting since the Civil War. The fleet, which could maneuver only as fast as its slowest member, the steam sloop *Shenandoah*, puffed along at four and a half knots. (Spain had four modern seagoing ironclads which could make nearly three times that speed.) In the end, perhaps, it was well that the President turned the *Virginius* affair over to the State Department for settlement.

There were few who would have guessed that twenty-five years later an American fleet would litter the beaches of Cuba with the burned and blasted wrecks of Spanish warships; that another American squadron would do the same thing in the distant Philippines; or that a decade after those victories, the most powerful fleet of battleships ever to circumnavigate the world would fly American colors.

Two then-obscure young men were to play major roles in this transformation. One, the only midshipman ever to skip plebe year at Annapolis—who, ironically, was to write of his naval career, "I believe I should have done better elsewhere"—was in 1873 a quiet, austere, and unhappy officer in command of the U.S.S. *Wasp*, a captured Civil War blockade-runner performing odd jobs for the ramshackle fleet of the South Atlantic Station. The other was the asthmatic son of a wealthy New York City family, just back from a sojourn in Germany and preparing for a gentleman's career at Harvard. Their names were Alfred Thayer Mahan and Theodore Roosevelt. It was Mahan whose

writings on the role of sea power in history would one day have such a far-reaching influence both at home and abroad. And it was his enthusiastic supporter, Roosevelt, who, first as Assistant Secretary of the Navy and then as President, would put the theories of that officer-scholar into practice.

Meanwhile the nation soon forgot its Caribbean misadventure: there was much more urgent business at hand. The problems of Reconstruction, the surge of population toward the West, the burgeoning of new industries, the ups and downs of the stock market, labor troubles, the social upheavals of immigration, and the scandals of the Grant administration seemed to leave little time for overseas affairs—or for the needs of a neglected navy.

While the navies of the major European powers relied increasingly on armored ships driven by steam, the American Navy, which had pioneered in both fields and which had more recent battle experience than all the rest put together, cruised under sail, in wooden ships. (There was even a move afoot to make all navy captains pay out of their own pockets for whatever coal their ships burned.) The promotion process stagnated; an Annapolis graduate might still be a lieutenant at the age of fifty. To make matters worse, the office of Secretary of the Navy was filled throughout the 1870's by political hacks. Grant's appointee, George M. Robeson, apparently managed to feather his nest with some $320,000 of Navy Department funds; a few years later, Richard W. Thompson of Indiana, who served under Hayes, visited a warship and exclaimed with some amazement, "The damn thing is hollow!"

"By the year 1880 the navy had fallen to a pitifully low ebb," noted Frank M. Bennett, the historian of the nineteenth-century American steam navy. "Repairs were no longer possible, for space for more patches was lacking upon almost every ship of ours then afloat. . . . A sense of humiliation dogged the American naval officer as he went about his duty in foreign lands; in the Far East, in the lesser countries along the Mediterranean Sea, and even in the sea ports of South America, people smiled patronizingly upon him and from a sense of politeness avoided speaking of naval subjects in his presence." That year there were thirty-eight admirals on the active list (with commands afloat for but six) and only thirty-nine ships. It was a situation that openly invited ridicule. In an Oscar Wilde comedy written at the time, an American lady who despaired of her country because it had neither curiosities nor ruins was consoled with heavy irony because "you have your manners and your navy."

But a change was in the air, though it would be a

long time before the officers and men of our patch-work naval forces would have tangible evidence of it. In 1880, when James Garfield was elected President, he chose William Hunt, a New Orleans Republican, as Secretary of the Navy. Hunt had long been friendly with two famous heroes of the Civil War, Admirals David Farragut and David Dixon Porter, and he had a lively interest in the service. He ordered a board, headed by Rear Admiral John Rodgers, to find out what was needed to rejuvenate the Navy.

The Rodgers board, apparently believing a serious question deserved a serious answer, urged that eighteen cruisers and fifty smaller ships be built at once—whereupon it was dismissed. Another board was appointed, which made recommendations that were less far-seeing but, for the moment, more practical. Following its suggestions, Congress provided for three steel cruisers and one dispatch boat, the latter a small ship useful for carrying messages.

Contracts for all four ships, the 4,500-ton *Chicago,* the 3,000-ton *Atlanta* and *Boston,* and the 1,500-ton *Dolphin,* were awarded to John Roach, a shipbuilder who was also a Republican wheel horse. In 1885 the first of the lot, the *Dolphin,* was completed; for months she lay alongside her pier, rakish in her standard navy black paint. But Congress and the Presidency had gone to the Democrats in 1884, and the *Dolphin* was rejected for an assortment of design and mechanical deficiencies. On the advice of friends in the Republican party, who perhaps thought they needed a martyr, Roach, instead of fighting the issue, went into bankruptcy. The *Atlanta, Boston,* and *Chicago* were taken over by the government half-built. Not until 1889 was the last of them completed and commissioned.

Eventually the *Dolphin* was accepted, and in 1888 she began a two-year cruise around the world. Men wilted inside her black steel hull as she passed through the tropics. Desperate for a remedy, her captain broke a century-old custom and painted his ship with white lead, thus cooling her interior by several degrees. The Navy Department copied his example; soon all new warships were coming out of their builders' yards in white. They were quite dashing, with ram bows decorated by gilt scrollwork or American shields, and upper works painted yellow ochre, much like today's Coast Guard cutters.

By the end of the decade the first of the Navy's armored cruisers, Roach's ships, were at sea, and more were being built. Gradually the old wooden fleet faded away. But American industry, though energetic and willing, had much to learn about building steel warships and supplying their needs. More important, no one in this country was yet competent to design a modern warship. The four ships that the unfortunate Roach built, for example, were all outfitted with a full set of sails in addition to reciprocating steam engines; the *Atlanta* and *Boston* were fitted with engines and boilers of a type already outmoded.

Disappointed with American plans, the Navy Department in the mid-eighties went to England and there obtained blueprints for the protected cruisers *Charleston* and *Baltimore,* and the second-class battleship *Texas.* The department was twice stung: the *Baltimore* proved satisfactory, but the blast from the *Texas'* two 12-inch guns, one on either side of the ship, tore away her upper works. The *Charleston's* engines were an amalgam of those of four other ships and the parts didn't fit; she never was made right. From then on, for better or worse, we depended almost exclusively on domestic talent for new designs.

Then, in 1890, Congress authorized the nation's first real battleships. The appropriation called for "seagoing, coast-line battleships," a grand contradiction, for a seagoing ship had to be a deep-draft, high-freeboard vessel with lots of room for coal, while a coast-line ship neither needed nor gained from any of these characteristics. At any event, the Navy took advantage of the confusion to build three of the finest warships of the age: *Indiana, Massachusetts,* and *Oregon.* Powerfully armed and heavily protected, they made only one concession to the "coast-line" part of the law: they were designed with a low freeboard.

The completion of the *Indiana*-class battleships, each weighing over ten thousand tons and armed with four 13-inchers, eight 8-inchers, and a variety of smaller guns, would signal a break with the past that was, in its own way, as revolutionary as the building of the first ironclads in the Civil War. Until now, Americans had imagined naval combat in terms of the heavy-footed, short-legged monitors guarding the home shores while swift cruisers like the newly commissioned *Columbia* and *Olympia* shot out of the mist to burn enemy—which naturally still meant English—merchant shipping. This was the formula that had worked to a degree in the special circumstances of 1812, when most of England's great navy had been occupied fighting the French. Under more normal conditions of war, however, it was likely to fail, as it had failed the Confederates in 1861. History showed that the chief business of a navy at war is to destroy or at least lock up the enemy's fleet. But big ships had always been needed to accomplish this end, and in 1890 that meant steel battleships.

Such was the persuasive argument of Captain Alfred Thayer Mahan, the sea-going intellectual who had been elevated from the humdrum of routine duty to head the newly established Naval War College in

Newport, Rhode Island. In 1886, his first year in the post, Mahan had delivered a series of lectures which, four years later, appeared as a book, *The Influence of Sea-power upon History, 1660–1783*. Though it was essentially a historical work, its implications were much broader, and it had a widespread influence both here and abroad. As the historian Louis M. Hacker has written:

... it was translated into all the important modern languages; it was read eagerly and studied closely by every great chancellory and admiralty; it shaped the imperial policies of Germany and Japan; it supported the position of Britain that its greatness lay in its far-flung empire; and it once more turned America toward those seas where it had been a power up to 1860 but which it had abandoned to seek its destiny in the conquest of its own continent.

Mahan's message—which in his day seemed revolutionary—was that a strong navy was the key to national power and security. And yet, only with the greatest reluctance did the Navy accept the formulations of this unsociable officer with the scholarly mind. ("It is not the business of a naval officer to write books," one hard-shell admiral once reminded Mahan when he asked that his next sea tour be put off until he had completed the volume he was then working on.) Gradually, however—and Mahan's influence is undeniable—the Navy underwent a fundamental transformation: an essentially provincial organization would one day become a sophisticated professional service which knew how to think in terms of war waged across the oceans and around the globe.*

If the *Indiana*-class battleships were models of advanced design, many of the ships which entered service in the nineties were obsolescent curiosities. Hardly any two were alike. There was the bizarre *Brooklyn*, with her huge beaked bow, tumble-home sides, and three slender smokestacks soaring a hundred feet above the furnace grates. There was the long, narrow *Vesuvius*, which fired shells filled with dynamite from three 15-inch pneumatic guns angling out of her fo'c'sle deck, and the *Katahdin*, armed with a formidable ram upon which she was to impale the foe. So that she might be invisible against her sea background she was painted green, and she could submerge till the deck was awash. Alas! She was too slow to catch any vessel with the wit to get out of the way.

Then there were the low, flat monitors—"about the shape of a sweet potato which has split in the boiling," wrote a future admiral, William S. Sims, who served for a time in one of them. Six in number, they had raft-like hulls little different from that of John Ericsson's

original *Monitor* of 1862. If one can accept the faintly cannibalistic idea of one ship absorbing another and quietly assuming her victim's identity, he can trace the history of most of these craft back to the Civil War.

The old *Monadnock*, for example, which shortly after the Civil War had smashed her way from east coast to west via the Horn in eight months, was found badly decayed and unseaworthy after a few years. "Repairs" at a private shipyard in San Francisco Bay were authorized in 1873, though work did not actually begin for another three years. By 1883, with the job still not done, the Navy seized the ship, towed her to the nearby Mare Island Navy Yard, and completed her—thirteen years later. When she poked her broad nose out of San Francisco Bay for the first time, in 1898, the only trace of the original *Monadnock* was the name; all the rest—hull, engines, boilers, and guns—was new. Unfortunately, a design that was good in 1873 had little to recommend it a quarter of a century later.

In spite of this lingering abundance of floating oddities and antiques, it was not a bad fleet, though hardly in a class with the navies of the major European powers. Nor did there seem any likelihood that it would be for years to come. As Admiral Bradley Fiske wrote, years later:

there was absolute conviction in the minds of everybody that the United States would never go to war again, and that our navy was maintained simply as a measure of precaution against the wholly improbable danger of our coast being attacked. It was not considered proper for a nation as great as ours not to have a fine navy; but the people regarded the navy very much as they regarded a beautiful building or fine natural scenery: a thing to be admired and to be proud of, but not to be used.

But a test of America's new navy came sooner than anyone expected. Affairs in Cuba had not improved since the days of the *Virginius* incident. In February, 1898, while on a visit to Havana, the battleship *Maine* blew up, killing 262 men. Spain frantically disclaimed responsibility (the cause of the explosion has never been satisfactorily determined) but to no avail. Two months later, the United States declared war. The fleet went into dull gray paint and loaded ammunition—which had been provided by the foresight of the energetic young New Yorker who was Assistant Secretary of the Navy, Theodore Roosevelt. His duty done, Roosevelt resigned to get into the fight with his own mounted regiment of cowboys and college boys.

In Europe, only the British favored an American victory, but they were not hopeful. As Commodore George Dewey led the Asiatic Squadron out of Hong Kong, the prevailing opinion of the Royal Navy officers was that the Americans were "a fine set of fellows, but unhappily we shall never see them again."

*Even in World War II Mahan's studies were influential in American naval thought, as Secretary of War Henry Stimson discovered when he frequently found himself confronted by that "dim religious world, in which Neptune was God, Mahan his prophet, and the United States Navy the only true Church."

It didn't work out that way. Dewey, with four cruisers, two gunboats, a Coast Guard cutter, and two supply ships, entered Manila Bay late in the night of April 30, exchanged a few shots with the forts at Corregidor, and early the next morning encountered Rear Admiral Don Patricio Montojo's squadron at Cavite, near the head of the bay. Montojo, backed by guns ashore, also had seven cruisers and gunboats, though his ships were older and smaller than Dewey's. The latter, taking time out in the midst of the action to serve his men breakfast, sank all of Montojo's ships without losing a man or a ship. Bradley Fiske, a veteran of the battle, noted that after Manila Bay, the British began to look upon the Americans as equals.

The Philippines, however, was a side show; Cuba remained at all times the chief theatre of war. By April, the Navy's half-dozen big ships in the Atlantic had been concentrated at Key West, and the Pacific Station's only battleship, the *Oregon*, was pounding up the east coast of South America at a steady eleven knots, en route to the Florida base.

Meanwhile, somewhere in the Atlantic, Rear Admiral Pasqual Cervera was at sea with the main Spanish squadron—four big armored cruisers accompanied by three torpedo boats. Panicking, the East Coast demanded naval protection. To give the appearance of a defense, Civil War monitors were hastily reconditioned and manned with naval militiamen. The public wanted more. So, despite Mahan's dictum that the battle fleet should never be broken up, it was. One half of our big ships were formed into the so-called Flying Squadron under Commodore Winfield Scott Schley in the *Brooklyn* and ordered north to Norfolk, to catch Cervera if he should try to shell coastal cities or beach resorts. It was an unwise move, for both the Flying Squadron and the ships remaining at Key West under Rear Admiral William T. Sampson in the armored cruiser *New York* were now outnumbered by the Spaniards. Luckily, however, Cervera had neither fuel nor ammunition to waste on civilian targets.

In time the Spanish admiral and six of his ships reached Santiago, on Cuba's southern coast, where they stopped for coal. After some hesitation, the North Atlantic Fleet, once again united under Sampson, gathered at the entrance to Santiago's little harbor and dared the foe to venture out. When nothing happened, a naval constructor named Richmond P. Hobson and seven volunteers attempted to trap Cervera by sinking an old merchant ship in the middle of Santiago's

TEXT CONTINUED ON PAGE 103
ILLUSTRATIONS CONTINUED ON FOLLOWING PAGES

Picture Credits: PP. 34–35, TOP LEFT, BUTTERFIELD COLLECTION, NEW YORK STATE HISTORICAL ASSOCIATION; BOTTOM LEFT, U.S. NAVAL ACADEMY MUSEUM; BOTTOM RIGHT, U.S. NAVAL INSTITUTE; OTHERS, AND ALL PHOTOS ON PP. 36–39, DETROIT PHOTOGRAPHIC COMPANY COLLECTION, LIBRARY OF CONGRESS. PP. 40–41, TOP, U.S. NAVAL ACADEMY MUSEUM; BOTTOM, MARINERS MUSEUM, NEWPORT NEWS, VA. PP. 42–43, CENTER LEFT, BOTTOM LEFT, BOTTOM RIGHT, U.S. NAVAL INSTITUTE; OTHERS, U.S. NAVY PHOTOS.

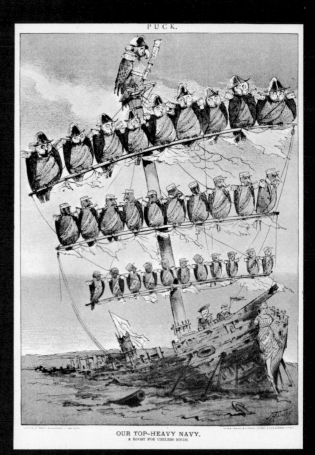

PUCK.

OUR TOP-HEAVY NAVY.
A ROOST FOR USELESS BIRDS.

1881: tumble-down ships and too many officers

New Era for the Navy

Alfred Thayer Mahan

The creation of a modern fleet was a slow and often uncertain process and was only accomplished through the perseverance of far-sighted men like the naval historian A. T. Mahan. In 1889, one of our first steel warships, the cruiser Chicago (above) was completed; she still carried sails. The design of the Brooklyn (right) may have been curious, but at least her builders trusted the steam engine. Not until the 1900's, however, when swift, powerful pre-dreadnought battleships like the Connecticut (below) began to appear, did the U.S. Navy finally come of age.

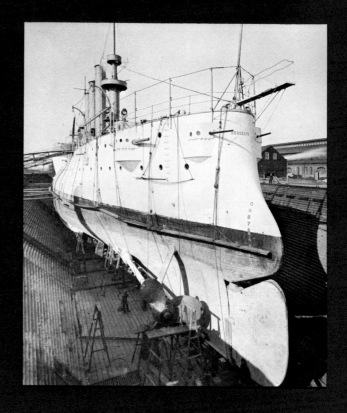

A flinty-eyed captain
posed at the wheel of his ship.

In the countenance of this chaplain,
there was the look of a Biblical prophet.

A sailor in a flat hat clowned for the camera.

A Prussian-style helmet was part of the dress uniform of shipboard marines.

Even the paymaster sported a cocked hat and a sword.

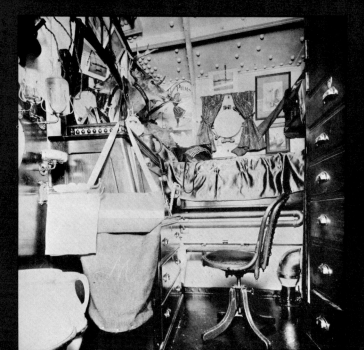

Two Ways

In the Navy of the 1880's and 1890's, the gulf between officers and enlisted men was always great, and seldom bridged. It was a matter not only of rank but also of background. Officers were generally of the middle class and graduates of the Naval Academy; most of the men were farm boys or immigrants, with little formal schooling. Living conditions were a plain indication of status. Though tiny and—in typical Victorian fashion—cluttered, the officer's stateroom at left had at least a modicum of comfort and privacy; the crowded, hammock-slung quarters of the ordinary sailor, like those

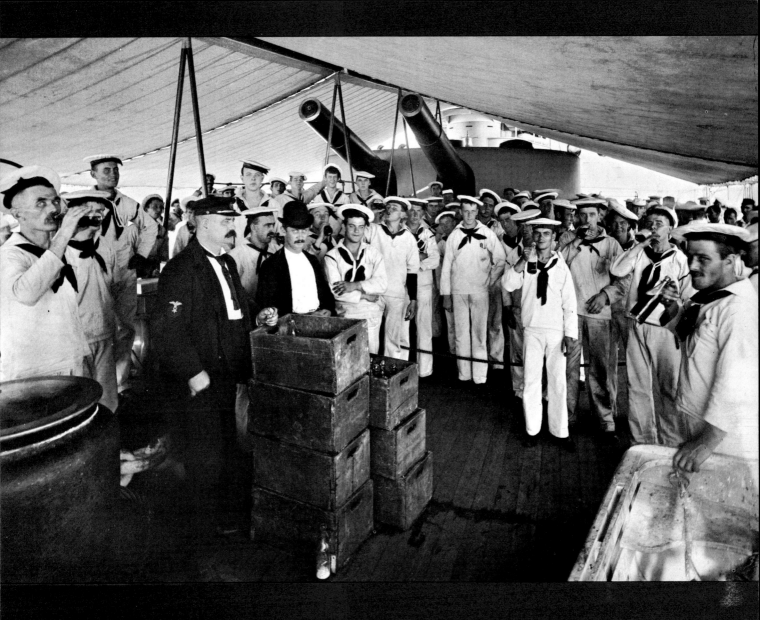

OF LIFE

shown at right, had none at all. Still, certain common pleasures were shared, if in different ways. Above left, officers in the wardroom of the U.S.S. Newark toast each other with champagne at a "wine mess"—a custom that was abolished in 1914 by Woodrow Wilson's temperance-minded Secretary of the Navy, Josephus Daniels. Before that time, sailors were also allowed an occasional beer ration— it is not hard to account for the smiles of the men of the U.S.S. Massachusetts, shown above bending an elbow in a moment of officially endorsed conviviality. Even to this day, the Navy remains dry.

THE GREAT WHITE

FLEET DEPARTS

Theodore Roosevelt regarded the Navy as a major instrument of national policy—the "big stick" that he displayed whenever necessary. During his two administrations (1901–1909), the United States became a great sea power, surpassed only by England and Germany. Nothing dramatized our newly acquired naval prowess—or our sudden emergence as a force in international politics—more than Roosevelt's decision in his second term to send the Atlantic fleet around the world. On December 16, 1907, as bands blared forth "The Girl I Left Behind Me," the sixteen battleships of the so-called Great White Fleet (below) sailed from Hampton Roads, Virginia. On the first leg of their momentous voyage, they were commanded by a tough old veteran of the Union navy in the Civil War, Rear Admiral Robley D. Evans, shown at left with the President.

AROUND THE WORLD

Ship's cutters race at Magdalena Bay, on Mexico's west coast.

There was dancing on shipboard at Sydney, Australia.

January, 1909; the fleet steams through the Suez Canal.

Curious Asians visit the battleship Connecticut.

In fourteen months, the Great White Fleet travelled 45,000 miles and visited six continents. Though its mission was peaceful, it was still the most formidable armada ever to undertake such a voyage—at a time when capital ships were considered a sure measure of national stature.

On February 22, 1909, as Theodore Roosevelt looked

Enthusiastic Japanese crowds welcome the American Navy in Yokohama.

Special trains took sightseeing Navy men across Ceylon.

"Shellbacks" initiate "pollywogs" at the equator.

on from the presidential yacht Mayflower, the Great White Fleet passed in review at the end of its journey.

One fine November day in 1848 a railroad locomotive christened the *Pioneer* chugged westward out of Chicago a distance of eight miles. It pulled only a single coach, a baggage car temporarily outfitted to carry a handful of prominent Chicagoans being treated to one of the first runs of the Galena & Chicago Union Railroad. Spotting a farmer driving an ox wagon filled with wheat and hides toward Chicago, two of the passengers purchased the goods and transferred them to the baggage car. The train then returned to its home city. This simple event foreshadowed the future course of Chicago's development: within twenty years the modest railroad comprising ten miles of track became the giant Chicago & North Western, one of the roads that made Illinois the nation's leader in railroad mileage; while the city itself grew tenfold to a population of 300,000. The inflow of wheat, which had begun when a group of men on a one-car train hauled a few bushels, amounted to tens of millions of bushels annually.

"Let the golden grain come, we can take care of it all," cried a Chicago newspaper of the 1850's. And come it did. Illinois was a major grain producer, and Chicago—"the New York of the West"—enjoyed a strategic location that made it the key transfer point for transcontinental trade. Systems like the Chicago & North Western and the Illinois Central funnelled in wheat, corn, and barley from the immense cereal carpet that lay to the city's west and northwest. During the sixties it became one of the world's primary grain markets; through the wonder of the telegraph, price fluctuations in the Chicago market were quickly communicated to the world and affected prices in New York and faraway Liverpool. At the center of these transactions stood the Chicago Board of Trade, the focal point for the buying and selling of grains, flour, and other foodstuffs. A contemporary called the Board "the Altar of Ceres," and the label was apt. Grain, and the money it might bring, was indeed a goddess to be worshipped by the restless merchants of the Board of Trade.

To accommodate the huge quantities which flowed in and out of Chicago there developed a most lucrative business, that of storing the grain in warehouses until it was sold and shipped east. (Railroad connections were such that direct shipments to eastern centers were difficult or impossible.) Known as grain elevators, the warehouses were skyscrapers able to hold 500,000 to 1,000,000 bushels in elongated, perpendicular bins that were mechanically loaded by the lifting up of dump buckets fastened to conveyor belts. Once the grain was deposited there, the warehousemen facilitated sales to merchants and speculators by issuing them receipts to represent the amount in storage. These receipts were regarded as

Grain elevators had false bottoms; freight rates had no ceilings. The farmers raised the roof, and government regulation crossed industry's threshold

MUNN v. ILLINOIS
A Foot in the

Ira Y. Munn

Door

By C. PETER MAGRATH

stable tokens of value comparable to bank bills; and presumably a warehouseman, like a banker, held a position of public trust demanding a high level of integrity. The presumption, however, proved to be quite unjustified.

The history of the great Chicago grain elevators is reflected in the rise and fall of Munn & Scott, a firm founded in Spring Bay, Illinois, in 1844. The two partners, Ira Y. Munn and George L. Scott, ran a small (about 8,000 bushels capacity) warehouse that served the north central part of the state. Munn, who was the firm's driving spirit, soon expanded his operations. Taking advantage of the opportunities presented by the growing commercial ascendancy of Chicago, he established a 200,000-bushel grain elevator there in 1856 under the name of Munn, Gill & Co. Two years later it became Munn & Scott, one of Chicago's thirteen elevator firms, which had a combined storage capacity of over four million bushels.

The next decade—one that belonged to America's capitalists—was enormously prosperous for Munn & Scott. They expanded to four elevators with a total capacity of 2,700,000 bushels; they could receive as many as 300,000 bushels daily and ship out twice that number. With success came power and prestige. Ira Munn emerged as a leading Chicago businessman; he was prominent in the affairs of the Board of Trade, serving as its president in 1860 and as president of the city's Chamber of Commerce in 1868. During the Civil War he participated conspicuously in activities supporting the Union cause. At the same time, good capitalist that he was, Ira Munn diversified his enterprises by engaging in wholesale grain speculation and by investing in newspapers and banks.

On the surface all seemed well for Munn & Scott, but they had their problems. These, in large measure, were of their own making; the age of enterprise was also an age of corruption, and the Chicago warehousemen were not at war with the spirit of their age. By 1868 Munn & Scott and four other firms dominated the field. They were interlocked in a business pool, each owning part interest in each of the others. They could thus fix prices and force farmers, who had to store their grain prior to sale, to pay high storage fees. There were cruder forms of chicanery. The warehousemen commonly made deals with the railway men whereby they were assured of receiving the grain carried by a particular line, regardless of the shipper's consignment. Munn & Scott, for instance, received most of their grain from the Chicago &

Some of the great Chicago grain elevators whose misuse brought on the struggle for government regulation of trade dominate this 1866 lithograph. One of Munn & Scott's elevators is seen at the right.

45

North Western. Another practice was to issue bogus receipts not backed by actual grain. Yet another favorite trick, performed with allied speculators, was to spread false rumors that the grain was spoiling; unsuspecting merchants would hasten to unload their grain receipts at depressed prices, thus setting up a juicy profit for the warehousemen.

While this sophisticated graft pleased the profiteers, it aroused its victims. As early as 1857, Chicago's grain merchants, acting through the Board of Trade, sought to impose a system of self-regulation upon the grain-elevator owners. Their aim was to get impartial inspectors into the warehouses to report on the condition and quantity of the grain in storage. A related objective was to make the Board a central registration agency which would record incoming shipments of grain and validate their sale, so as to eliminate the practice of issuing bogus receipts. The warehousemen naturally resisted, claiming that as private owners they had an inherent right to exclude outside parties from their property. Since the elevator proprietors also had representation on the Board of Trade, they were usually able to turn the regulatory proposals into meaningless compromises. The upshot was the semblance but not the substance of regulation: grain weighers who were in the employ of the warehousemen; Board inspectors whose admission into the elevators depended upon the owners' good will and who were vulnerable to bribes; and unverifiable reports, filed by the warehousemen, which were as worthless as many of their grain receipts.

The Munn & Scott firm was both a prime cause of complaints and a leader in the fight against effective control by the Board. In 1861, after warehouse "wheat doctors" had camouflaged a huge quantity of spoiled grain and mixed it with good grades, open charges of fraud were voiced. The Board appointed an investigating committee, but by tacit agreement its report was suppressed. When Joseph Medill's crusading Chicago *Tribune* suggested that the report had been shelved because it incriminated many elevator men, Munn & Scott succeeded in getting *Tribune* reporters expelled from Board meetings. Similar newspaper charges hinting at Munn & Scott frauds appeared in 1865; another public furor followed, but the lax inspection procedures remained unchanged.

Four years later almost all of Chicago's receivers, shippers, and dealers united in demanding a system of real inspection. The immediate cause was a raise in storage rates and the imposition of an extra charge for grain that spoiled while in storage. New Board regulations designed to eliminate fraudulent issues of grain receipts were adopted early in 1870; once again the warehousemen, including Munn & Scott, asserted their right to control matters within their own elevators. The

An Unforeseen Collaboration

Left to right: Justices Bradley, Field, Miller, Clifford; Chief

Public feeling against the railroads' exorbitant freight rates was sharply prodded by the Patrons of Husbandry, or Grangers. Organized in 1867 as an agrarian social society, it grew rapidly into a powerful political force against the economic malpractices of railroads and middlemen. By 1873, when economic depression had intensified their woes, the Grangers had founded scores of papers and journals to promote their complaints. The cartoon at left, captioned The Grange Awakening the Sleepers, *puns on a familiar synonym for railroad crossties. Some big-city papers, notably the Chicago* Tribune, *edited by Joseph Medill (right), helped by campaigning vigorously for state regulation of grain elevators. Eventually the Supreme Court of 1877 (below) sided with the Grangers, thus belying its conservative looks.*

Justice Waite; Justices Swayne, Davis, Strong, and Hunt.

fight intensified. Elections for Board of Trade offices in the spring of 1870 split the membership into two factions—one supported the warehousemen; the other, which won most of the positions, insisted that their power be broken.

Businessmen are not customarily champions of governmental regulation, but the warehouse situation had become intolerable. The conduct of complex business relationships, after all, depends in significant part on mutual trust. Unable to control the warehousemen, the Board of Trade turned to the state, asking that Illinois subject them to public regulation. It was necessary, declared the retiring Board president in 1870, to destroy "a monopoly highly detrimental to every interest of the city." Joseph Medill, whose newspaper made warehouse regulation its cause, put it more colorfully when he described the warehousemen as "rapacious, blood sucking insects." These complaints went before the state's constitutional convention of 1869–1870, then in session. The result was one of those strange yet almost typical alliances of American politics: a temporary pact between two normally opposed interests, the grain merchants and the grain producers.

The farmer-merchant alliance was an unusually strange one for 1870 because that year found the midwestern farmer in the grip of depression. Beyond a doubt, the economic balance of the post-Civil War period was heavily weighted against the American farmer. Between 1861 and 1865 he had rapidly expanded production to meet burgeoning needs, but the postwar market absorbed only part of his fantastic output of wheat, corn, and other grains. The farmer, moreover, sold in an unprotected world market at a time of falling prices; wheat, which sold at $1.45 a bushel in 1866, dropped to 76 cents within three years. As prices dropped, the value of money appreciated, and the farmers, who had borrowed in the wartime flush of inflationary optimism, had to meet debts with a scarce and hard-earned currency. Manufacturers, by contrast, were protected by a high tariff which pushed up the cost of the farmers' tools and domestic necessities.

The farmers of the West and Midwest had yet another grievance which became a focus of all their discontents —the great railroad systems whose shiny rails crisscrossed the farm country. No one had welcomed the coming of the railroad more than the western farmer, since it opened up new markets for his products and made farming feasible in otherwise remote areas. Many had mortgaged their property to buy railroad shares; others had cheerfully accepted high local taxes to finance the bonds that lured the iron horse into their territory.

Unfortunately, the harvest was a bitter one. Once established, the railroads treated their clientele with disdain. Company officials were overbearing, charged exorbitant rates, and discriminated in favor of large shippers, who received special discounts. Precisely because the railroads were essential, they could act arrogantly; in any given area a single line usually enjoyed a monopoly and thus could charge as much as the traffic would bear. The railroads, of course, defended their rates as moderate, sufficient only to make good on the immense speculative risks they had undertaken. The farmers were unimpressed. To them the dominant fact was that freight costs ate up a frightful percentage of their income. Sometimes they were even reduced to burning their corn as fuel rather than shipping it to market at a loss.

Their profound discontent soon led them to organize. Oddly, what became the major vehicle for agrarian protest had its start as a fraternal order intended to end the farmers' isolation from social and educational opportunities. In 1867 an idealistic government clerk in Washington, Oliver Hudson Kelley, singlehandedly founded the National Grange of the Patrons of Husbandry. At first his organization existed more on paper than in reality, but Kelley was an indefatigable worker—and also a shrewd observer. He broadened the Grange's appeal by making its primary objectives co-operative purchasing and the control of monopolies. These tactics paid off, and the Grange spread like prairie wildfire. It soon blanketed the entire nation, reaching its peak in 1874 when representatives of some 800,000 farmers convened in St. Louis to proclaim "the art of agriculture" as "the parent and precursor of all arts, and its products the foundation of all wealth."

Although "the Grange" became a synonym for all the agrarian movements of the seventies, there were other highly vocal farmers' associations which antedated the Patrons of Husbandry, and which intervened in politics throughout the Midwest. All shared the same goals: elimination of the middleman's profits, lowered interest charges, and, most insistently, railroad rate regulation. "We were all grangers," a farmer later recalled. "I never belonged to the order but I was a granger just the same."

In Illinois the farmers scored one of their first successes when they joined with Chicago's merchants in getting the state's constitutional convention to authorize railroad and warehouse regulation. Like the Board of Trade, Illinois farmers had just cause for wanting to see the elevators controlled. Typically, a farmer might ship 1,000 bushels of wheat to Chicago, but receive a warehouse receipt for only 950. After paying costly storage charges, he might be told that his grain was "heating" and that, to avoid a complete disaster, he should sell his receipt to the warehouseman at a loss of 10 cents per bushel. Later, the hapless farmer would learn that his grain, perfectly sound, had been sold at a nice profit. But beyond their joint desires to clean up a dirty business, both farmers and merchants were interested in comprehensive regulation. The Board of Trade wanted to make normal business relationships possible; the farmers wanted a stringent limitation on the rates charged by railroads and warehouses.

Acting in response to these pressures, the 1871 legislature passed laws forbidding railroad discriminations and prescribing maximum freight and passenger rates. The warehousemen's fraudulent practices were outlawed, storage rates were limited, and a Board of Railroad and Warehouse Commissioners was created to enforce the regulations.

Enforcement, however, was not easy. The warehousemen proclaimed the law unconstitutional and ignored it. Munn & Scott refused to take out the required license and kept the state-appointed registrar of grain out of their elevators. The state then sued the firm; but the trial proceedings were delayed because of the mass destruction of records by Chicago's Great Fire of 1871. In July, 1872, the state won a judgment of $100; Munn & Scott promptly appealed to the Illinois Supreme Court.

Meanwhile, however, through a series of related events, the downfall of Munn & Scott was beginning. Despite the state regulation (which at first had no practical impact), the Board of Trade continued to seek inspection of the warehouses during 1871 and 1872. Some elevators co-operated with Board inspectors in measuring their grain, but Munn & Scott remained defiant. Finally, in 1872, the firm consented to admit inspectors. It requested, however, that its elevators be inspected last in order to give it time to consolidate its grains and to avoid any implication of particular mistrust of Munn & Scott. The Board agreed, and the firm put the time to good use—flooring over the tops of several bins in one large elevator and covering the false bottoms with grain so as to give the illusion of full bins. The inspectors were fooled until an employee divulged the secret, and it was learned that Munn & Scott grain receipts totaling 300,000 bushels were not backed by grain.

Deplorable as the corruption was, its disclosure merely confirmed what had long been suspected. More immediately damaging were Munn & Scott's financial misadventures in the summer of 1872. Along with three other speculators, the firm attempted to corner all the wheat pouring into Chicago, hoping to dictate its ultimate price in world markets. For a while the corner worked, as Munn & Scott made huge purchases. The heavy buying, however, pushed the price of wheat so high that the farmers, who normally held some grain in reserve in the hope that its value would rise, shipped their surplus to market. This was the crucial stage, for

CONTINUED ON PAGE 88

Voyage Pittoresque
AUX ÉTATS-UNIS DE l'AMÉRIQUE.
Par Paul Svignine
En 1811, 1812, ET 1813.

Paul Svinin

Not all Russian diplomats in America have had ice water in their veins and a ready "Nyet" upon their lips. One of the first of them left an illustrated record, subsequently "lost" for more than a century, which pictured a people he liked and a land he admired

By MARSHALL B. DAVIDSON

The path of the Russian diplomat in America, like that of his American counterpart in Russia, is far from smooth. He must of necessity follow every tortuous twist and turn of international politics, and upon his shoulders he must carry the crushing burden of history. This has been particularly true since the Soviet Revolution of 1917, and the diplomat's situation has grown even worse since the freeze in Russian-American relations that followed the brief thaw at Yalta.

It was not always so. One of the first Russians to come to America in an official capacity was an urbane and talented young man of twenty-four, Paul Svinin (to give his name its simplest Anglicized form), who joined his country's first permanent embassy to the United States in Philadelphia in the late autumn of 1811 as secretary to the consul general, Andrey Yakovlevich Dashkov. Americans knew very little about the imperial Russia that had sent him; in the next two years Svinin did all he could to build up in their minds a favorable image of his native land, and subsequently to convey to his own countrymen some of the personal enthusiasm he developed for the nation to which he had been assigned. His spirited and informed commentaries—and his portfolio of water colors, from which those on the following pages have been selected—give a rare and valuable picture of a new republic and its people.

Such reputation as Russia had here when Svinin arrived was hardly favorable. In the early spring of 1779, when Americans were struggling for their independence, a report had reached Detroit by way of Montreal that 12,000 Russian troops—hired by George III from Catherine the Great—had landed at New York. The rumor turned out to be false, for though the King had indeed asked for Russian mercenaries, Catherine refused to become involved. On the other hand, when in 1780 the Americans in turn had tried to win her active support, she was even less responsive than she had been to the plea of their ex-king. Moreover, she refused to recognize America's claim to independence until after England did, and when in the tragic "final" partition of Poland in 1795 her troops wounded and captured Thaddeus Kosciusko, the great Polish patriot so gratefully remembered here for his service in our own war for freedom, Americans were outraged. Catherine died the following year, and Philip Freneau, poet, editor, and irrepressible patriot, dashed off an epitaph which, with more passion than judgment, gave voice to America's indignation:

> She would have sent her Tartar bands
> To waste and ravage Gallic lands,
> She would have sent her legions o'er,
> Columbia! to invade your shore!

There were those in Russia who were also disenchanted with Catherine's autocratic rule, notably an intellectual elite who found in what they had heard of the American revolutionary experience a pattern for their own political and social ideals, and a strong contradiction to the unfortunate realities of Russian life. Foremost among this group, although an aristocrat and a member of the imperial Russian government under Catherine, was Alexander Radishchev, who penned a long ode to the young republic in the New World. For this and other libertarian sentiments Radishchev earned a ten-year exile in Siberia, from which he returned unregenerate to write further passionate eulogies of American freedom, justice, and humanitarianism. He concluded, however, that Russians did not have enough evidence to draw an "exact" picture of the American scene.

Almost a quarter of a century passed before they would have that evidence, for in the years following the Treaty of Paris the United States withdrew from "foreign entanglements" and Russia was preoccupied with problems on the Continent. As so often since, it was mutual self-interest—each wanted support from the other in meeting troubles arising out of the Napoleonic Wars—that drew the two nations together. In October of 1809, John Quincy Adams was dispatched to St. Petersburg (see "The Yankee and the Czar" in the February, 1958, AMERICAN HERITAGE); Dashkov (and later Paul Svinin) was sent to America.

Svinin was a well-educated youth, master of several Western languages, and as a member of the Russian Foreign Office he was already widely travelled in Europe. He was also an artist of academic rank. Just two or three days before his departure for America he had been elected to membership in the Academy of Fine Arts at St. Petersburg, where only a few years earlier he had been a student. Some idea of the unchangeable tides of taste in Russia can be gathered from a description of his membership-winning canvas: "The celebrated hero, Suvorov, resting, after a battle, on straw, by a stream, in a tent made of cloaks fastened to Cossack spears, with a military camp and groups of horses, Cossacks, soldiers and Turkish prisoners filling the background, as morning breaks and the dawn begins to gild Nature." Change the characters into deserving proletarians and their enemies, and it would probably still win a Soviet prize as an example of solid contemporary art.

As an intellectual and a seasoned traveller Svinin well knew what "ridiculous wonders and strange falsehoods" were circulating abroad about Russia and Russians, and he must have quickly realized that his country had not enjoyed a very good press in America. He immediately set about putting the record straight. Within a few months of his arrival he had two articles published in *The Philadelphia Port Folio*, then a leading American periodical. One was a eulogy of his sovereign, Czar Alexander I, grandson of Catherine; the other a sympathetic account of the Cossacks, and each had an illustration after a drawing by the author. Before he returned to Russia he also had published in Philadelphia a book that gave Americans a more detailed report on his native land. Like America, he explained, Russia was rapidly transforming a wilderness into attractive cities, and it, too, was rising to new and great importance in the world.

Svinin was neither the first nor the last to point out the resemblances between the bear and the eagle, but some of his arguments were unique. Like America, he observed, Russia was an asylum for the unfortunate and the persecuted, and like Americans, Russians practiced complete religious freedom. Witness to those facts was that, although immigrants from a dozen other European lands had fled to America, no Russians had found it necessary to leave the benign jurisdiction of the Czar. Later and elsewhere he explained this by pointing out that the Russian peasant who felt oppressed by the injustices of the Russian agrarian order or by the religious persecutions of the Orthodox Church could always find refuge by fleeing to remote parts of the vast empire, to Siberia if need be, without having to cross the Atlantic.

For his own favorable prejudices toward America, Svinin was very probably indebted to such writings as Radishchev's. In any event, he found almost everything about the young nation admirable, except the Philadelphia summers, which then, as ever, were almost intolerable. His official duties apparently did not begin to fill his time. For one thing, aside from a few colleagues in the foreign service, he found no Russians in the United States, although he discovered a few impostors who for "credit or speculation" claimed to be Russians. For twenty months this cosmopolitan traveller roamed about the eastern seaboard, from Maine to Virginia, interviewing people of importance and men in the streets and shops, attending learned assemblies, art openings, camp meetings, and Indian tribal ceremonies, and sketching what particularly caught his eye.

His anecdotal approach to art was well suited to graphic journalism. He was reporting for a remote and completely alien, but curious, audience, and he caught some likenesses of the American scene overlooked by other reporting artists of the time. His fine close-ups of life in the streets of Philadelphia and on the Hudson River have the candid, romantic realism that made Currier and Ives lithographs so popular a half century later, and they were unique in their day. Only six of them were reproduced during Svinin's own lifetime. In his last published work he made casual reference to the portfolio he had compiled, at which point it disappeared from all notice for almost a century. So, to all intents, did his writings on the New World. The dramatic and al-

most simultaneous rediscovery of both in the 1920's (see page 52), was one of those "angelical conjunctions of events" (as Cotton Mather would have said) that practically never happens in the course of historical research.

Svinin was a highly competent observer. He warned his readers not to be misled by English and French accounts of the American Revolution. Conditions changed too rapidly in this new country, he cautioned, to permit any lasting and valid analysis. His own sympathies for what he was reporting, however, often weighted his judgment and led to comments that would seem incongruous from a latter-day Russian visitor. The fruits of private enterprise he found omnipresent and impressive. Just before his arrival, a New York merchant, one "Ivan Astor," whom he subsequently interviewed, had sent an overland expedition to the Pacific Northwest for a harvest of furs, and two ships around the Horn to join the land force at an appointed rendezvous. "This expedition will cost him 250,000 rubles," Svinin reported. "What an enterprise for a private citizen! May it be crowned with success."

He was struck by the remarkable growth of public works—canals, roads, and, particularly, handsome bridges, some of which were "truly worthy of the glorious age of the Roman empire"—that were being engineered and promoted almost entirely without government aid. In this respect Robert Fulton's steamboats, which he had watched in their early trials on the Hudson River, fascinated Svinin. The spectacle of the *Paragon*, Fulton's third Hudson River boat, with its polished and gleaming accommodations for 150 passengers—with wine, food, and even ice cream for the most fastidious— carried Svinin to heights of exultation. Soon, he prophesied, such craft would be crossing oceans and bringing back treasures from all parts of the world. The profits from this happy invention, he noted, were already attractive—each boat returned about forty thousand rubles a year—and he tried to secure for himself a monopoly for building them in Russia, where they would, among other things, release the Volga boatmen from their endless toil along the river and put them to endless toil behind the plough, where they would do more good. But nothing came of this private enterprise.

The inventiveness of Americans in general, an inevitable consequence of insufficient manpower in a land of enormous resources and limited capital, he found remarkable. Everything from sawing rocks and making bricks to cobbling shoes and milling flour, he said extravagantly, was done by machine. Yet almost everyone worked hard. Money was the American's god, but piety and the natural wealth of the land sustained his morals.

In spite of barbaric electioneering practices and political party feuds, the nation's laws were wise and just,

TEXT CONTINUED ON PAGE 107
A PORTFOLIO OF WATER COLORS CONTINUES ON THE FOLLOWING PAGES

51

The first Russian to publish an eyewitness report of the American scene was Paul Svinin, a graduate member of the Academy of Fine Arts in St. Petersburg and a widely travelled polyglot in his country's foreign service. During his stay of twenty months in the United States, from the autumn of 1811 to the late summer of 1813, Svinin compiled a portfolio of fifty-two water colors of American subjects. In 1814, as he paused in London en route to Russia, Svinin received "advantageous offers" to publish his sketches together with an account of his experiences in the new republic. But the outspoken anti-American bias of the English publisher was so completely contrary to the Russian artist's own sentiments that he rejected the proposal. Rather, he averred, his own fatherland should "reap the first fruits of my labors." His *Picturesque Voyage in North America* was in fact published in St. Petersburg in 1815, almost immediately after his return to Russia, and he wrote other reports in subsequent years. Of the water colors, however, only a very few were reproduced in his own lifetime—in Russia—and upon his death in 1839 the portfolio disappeared from view for almost a century. So to all intents did the published accounts of his American experiences, which apparently remained completely unknown in this country.

In the early 1920's the water colors returned to the United States in the luggage of an American Red Cross worker who had purchased them while serving in Russia during the agonizing days that followed the Bolshevist revolution. They entered the collection of R. T. Haines Halsey, an American collector, who recognized them as a unique and unheard-of graphic account of our republic in its early years. By an unparalleled coincidence, at almost the same time Avrahm Yarmolinsky and H. M. Lydenburg of the New York Public Library, on a buying trip in Russia, stumbled across a copy of Svinin's published report on America in which six of the water colors were rather poorly reproduced. A reference to the "lost" portfolio turned up in another of Svinin's books, and while Dr. Yarmolinsky from the New York library canvassed the museums of Russia to locate the portfolio, Halsey, not far from Yarmolinsky's base in New York, was making equally determined efforts to identify and fill in the background of the hitherto unknown artist.

Inevitably the two men met, and the separate halves of the story were pieced together. Almost everything that is known of Svinin was brought to light by Dr. Yarmolinsky; most of the quotations in the accompanying article are from his published translations of Svinin's writings. The Russian diplomat's charming water colors are now in the Metropolitan Museum of Art, in New York.

The New Nation

Through Russian Eyes

Svinin's water color of the Trenton Diligence is the only intimate view we have of early stagecoach travel in America. He was rhapsodic over Robert Fulton's new steamboats and convinced that they were quickly rendering the land vehicles obsolescent. But for years still to come, coaching over breakneck roads, "crushed, shaken, thrown about . . . and bumped," remained one of the hardships of touring America.

Life and Limb

Svinin's travels in America took him from Maine to Virginia and at least as far west as Niagara Falls. Although his written reports did not mention how he got from one place to another, his water colors provide an eloquent commentary on his adventures en route. The hardships of inland travel reached a point of downright peril at some places where roads were interrupted by large streams, rivers, and tidal waters, and where travellers, along with their vehicles and justifiably nervous horses, were crowded aboard flimsy ferries. Even such a redoubtable hero as General Horatio Gates had lost courage a few years earlier when he saw how shaken the incoming passengers were from their passage across the Hudson River. At right center, Svinin depicts a crossing of the Susquehanna River at Wright's Ferry. The ferrymen in the sketch above are identifiable as Osage Indians from portraits drawn earlier by Saint-Mémin; the figure shown between them may represent Svinin himself. At bottom, the sailing packet Mohawk of Albany beats its way up the Hudson River past the Palisades. In the wayside-inn scene on the opposite page, one of the merrymakers, whip in hand and puffing on a stogie, may by those appurtenances be identified as the driver of one of the Conestoga wagons parked before the door of the inn. As the English blockade during the War of 1812 diverted intercoastal traffic from the seas, Conestogas trucked freight overland.

City Life

At the time of Svinin's visit, Philadelphia was still the largest, most impressive American city. The sawyers above ply their trade before Latrobe's Bank of Pennsylvania, which the artist considered the handsomest building in the country.

An oyster vender peddles his wares at night to a gay group in front of the Chestnut Street Theatre. The carved figures of Comedy and Tragedy by William Rush, "the father of American sculpture," can be dimly seen in the niches on the façade.

The Brief Past - the Long Future

Although he was only in his early twenties, Svinin was probably the most widely travelled artist to report on America up to the time of his visit. Starting as a teen-age "Translator and Cavalier of the State Board of Foreign Affairs," he had already voyaged widely: to Denmark and England, Sicily and Greece, Portugal, Spain, France, Germany, and other lands. But he found fresh interest in virtually every aspect of the American scene. At Mount Vernon he visited the tomb of "the immortal Washington" (left), whose name was so dear to liberal Russians. On his journeys about the countryside he was constantly reminded of the rate at which the new republic was developing. His sketch of an unidentified town along the Mohawk River (below) accents his observation that everywhere he went, "more like a dream than a reality," cities of unpredictable size were springing up out of the primeval forest.

New York, Svinin accurately predicted, would
soon assume commanding importance; among other
landmarks there he pictured the curious "churn"
flagstaff structure at the Battery (above), which
served both as a gazebo for those who turned
their spyglasses seaward and as a refresh-
ment stand for those who favored cakes and beer.

The Pennsylvania Hospital in Philadelphia
(right) remained a monument to the progressive,
humane spirit of the Quaker City. In Russia, as
elsewhere abroad, the Quakers enjoyed the
highest respect. Alexander Radishchev, the
first noble Russian radical and friend of the
young United States, had hailed the Quakers
as those "peaceful haters of bloodshed." Shortly
after Svinin's return to Russia, Czar Alexander I, "bathed with tears," embraced and kissed
a pair of Quakers whom he had invited to his
palace for a discussion of humanitarian reforms.

As a native of a land of religious conformity, Svinin found the variety of religious professions in America startling. Even members of the same household might be of different persuasions, he observed, and still live together amicably, which, he concluded, "redounds to the credit of the American Government and of the character of the Americans."

Contrasted with the staid ritual of the Orthodox Church into which he had been born, the camp meetings and revival ceremonies of the Methodists seemed almost frighteningly noisy and violent. After attending an exceptionally emotional Negro service, Svinin reflected that only a beneficent spirit could have delivered him through the excited crowd of worshippers who "thronged even the entrance to the church" (above). One day he witnessed an outdoor Anabaptist ceremony (right above), in which "these [initiates] step solemnly

Religion: Freedom in Diversity

into the river, the while a choir sings." A Quaker family strolling past the Arch Street Meeting House (right) suggests the sober mood of a Philadelphia Sunday. "One does not see a single smile," Svinin wrote, "—it is as though the city were in mourning." Beneath the bonnets of the Quakeresses, however, he detected "the seductive charm of their blue eyes and fair tresses." The ladies had, he noticed, "fine figures and small feet."

The Wonders—and Terrors—of Nature

The natural spectacles of America were to Svinin, as to so many other visitors, a frequent source of wonder. The scenes above picture the sudden violence of a tornado that whipped a placid, tidy landscape (left) into an unrecognizable shambles (right). He went to see Natural Bridge, Virginia (below)—"two tall mountains . . . joined by a perfect granite arch suspended in the air," as he reported it. "What an object for the naturalist! What a field for the conjectures of the philosopher!" Niagara Falls, which he pictured by moonlight (opposite), all but overwhelmed the artist. "The indomitable river that hurls itself with so much fury across thousands of granite cliffs . . . the deafeningly thundering roar, the shaking rocks," all filled him with visions of unutterable might and mystery.

"Jeff, it's up to you!"

By FINIS FARR

When the Negro Jack Johnson fought Jim Jeffries at Reno in 1910, more than the world heavyweight championship seemed at stake. To the many alarmed by Johnson's unsavory reputation, Jeffries seemed nothing less than the "Great White Hope"

When Jack Johnson beat Tommy Burns for the world heavyweight professional boxing championship at Sydney, Australia, on December 26, 1908, he became the first Negro to hold the highest title in boxing, with all its symbolic and economic importance. It was not a popular victory. Perhaps the white public at this period would have accepted a modest and respectable Negro as champion, but never one like Johnson. A former drifter who had seen the inside of countless jails throughout the United States, he had begun his pugilistic career fighting in barrooms and back streets. He cut a figure in international café society, was frequently drunk and in trouble for speeding in his racing car, played the bull fiddle, and made no secret of his liking for handsome blonde white women of the sort who generally travelled with boxers, jockeys, and criminals. So it was that the famous writer Jack London, covering the Burns fight for the New York *Herald,* ended his dispatch with the appeal that James J. Jeffries, who had retired undefeated in 1905, should "emerge from his alfalfa farm and remove the golden smile from Jack Johnson's face. Jeff, it's up to you!"

Thirty years old when he won the title, the Texas-born Johnson was a superb fighter—some authorities say the best who ever came along. It seemed so, after he defeated Burns, although other powerful Negroes like Sam Langford, whom he had previously beaten, might have made trouble had Jack allowed any of them a return match. But his virtuosity was now so great that he could show disrespect both to opponents and audiences in a way that set the brutal fight crowds gibbering with rage. In vain were the "White Hopes" sent against him. The burly Al Kaufman, who was taller and heavier, could do nothing. Victor McLaglen, the future movie star, was badly beaten. Capable boxers like Tony Ross, Billy Delaney, and Philadelphia Jack O'Brien were helpless against him, and the middleweight champion, Stanley Ketchel, was floored in twelve rounds. There grew up a general belief that only Jim Jeffries could put Johnson on his back. Flour-

ishing in a thousand barrooms, the desire to see the Negro defeated at last became so intense that it focussed attention on Jeffries like the converging of the sun's rays through a burning glass.

Born in 1875, James Jackson Jeffries had grown up in the boiler-making trade in California and turned to the ring as a young man. In 1899, after only twelve professional fights, he won the world's heavyweight championship by knocking out Bob Fitzsimmons. When Jeffries retired six years later, he had never been knocked off his feet. After an elimination bout, which he refereed, he conferred the title on Marvin Hart, who promptly lost it to Burns. An awesome figure in retirement, Jeffries had ballooned to a weight of more than three hundred pounds, but retained his great strength, and could still break any man's grip with either hand. He had the myth-making quality of a real folk hero; people believed, for example, that he had cured himself of pneumonia by drinking a case of whiskey in two days. It was widely held that he had a mortal hatred for Johnson, and bartenders told steady customers that if the fight could be arranged, Jeffries would "probably kill the Negro."

Though flattered by the general confidence in his strength and skill, Jeffries had doubts as to the wisdom of returning to the ring. All the same, there was something hypnotic in the way the sporting public pressed its consensus upon him by assuming that the match was made. "Proud to shake the fist that's going to kill Jack Johnson!" a barfly would say, grabbing Jeffries' huge paw. "When's it going to be, Jeff?" Hundreds of letters from strangers came into his California home, the writers telling Jeffries of their certainty that it was his duty to fight Johnson and his destiny to hand him

Finis Farr's account of the Johnson-Jeffries fight is taken from his new book, Black Champion: the Life and Times of Jack Johnson, *to be published by Charles Scribner's Sons. A writer who resolutely refuses to be stereotyped, Mr. Farr has published a much-acclaimed biography of Frank Lloyd Wright and is now at work on a book about Margaret Mitchell.*

ILLUSTRATED FOR AMERICAN HERITAGE BY FRANK MULLINS

the biggest defeat in the history of the boxing ring.

Early in 1909, Jeffries decided he must take inventory of his life and career, look into the business aspects of a match with Johnson, and decide what to do about it. He appointed a sporting San Francisco hatter named Sam Berger as his personal manager, and sent him to hold confidential talks with Johnson's representatives. These preliminary negotiations took place in various Chicago and San Francisco hotels; their successful concealment from the press showed that Johnson, who had been called crazy over publicity, could keep a close mouth when it suited him.

Roving in the hotel barrooms, reporters sensed the drama of high contracting parties moving to a deal. Lacking information from the principals, they circulated rumors that Johnson was agreeing to throw the fight to Jeffries for a large sum. How this money was to be raised no one seemed to know, still less why Johnson would bargain away his earning power. Johnson and Jeffries made a private agreement to fight. The exact date on which they came to the decision still is not known, but it can be deduced that Jeffries made a conditional agreement late in the spring of 1909, the condition being his ability to get down to 227 pounds without ruining his health. With this problem in mind he set out for the weight-reducing headquarters of the time, the mineral baths at Carlsbad in northwest Bohemia (now part of Czechoslovakia). Here he proposed to consult the medical staff; he would begin heavy training only if they said it was safe. And at Carlsbad Jeffries received final proof that the world took it for granted he would destroy Jack Johnson.

It happened that King Edward VII of England was a frequent patron of Carlsbad, finding the waters beneficial and the place convenient for his attentions to a number of ladies in the spa's luxurious hotels. Thus it was not surprising that on his first morning in town Jeffries encountered the King taking his usual walk. Edward VII was identifiable—in spite of the dark glasses over his brandied and protuberant eyes—by the familiar gray Homburg, "torpedo" beard, and projecting paunch. The lantern-jawed Jeffries was also a recognizable celebrity because of his great height and bulk, and the King hailed him in his characteristic wheezing and guttural tones.

"Hello there, Jim Jeffries!" said the genial monarch. "Going to fight the blackfellow, eh? Jolly good! I say it's great luck to meet you. I hear all Americans know about furs. Come along and help me pick out a few."

With that, the King seized Jeffries' arm and pulled him into a furrier's shop. Jeffries was strait-laced where women were concerned, and looked on in disapproval as the fawning proprietor laid out skin after skin; the King demanded his opinion of each item. At last Edward bought five thousand dollars' worth of silver fox scarves and allowed Jeffries to go. Later in the week the Carlsbad doctors told him he could safely reduce to ring weight within a year. He took the waters, and then travelled back to the United States at a leisurely pace, sending word to Johnson early in October that all they needed now was an acceptable promoter and financier.

While this matter was being settled, Johnson continued to cut a fashionable figure with his dozens of well-tailored suits, his handmade shoes, his racing cars, and his women—who always seemed to be white, blonde, and not given to formality of manner. Today they would be called "models" or "starlets," but they were in fact prostitutes. Johnson paraded them with ostentation, thus arousing disapproval not only because the racial mix irritated both white people and conservative Negroes, but also because his flouting of morality stimulated the reformers and stirred them to action against drinking, gambling, and prostitution. Johnson made things bad for everybody, and so was detested not only in Sunday schools but among the host of pimps, whores, gamblers, distillers, brewers, and their customers, who believed that where business and pleasure were concerned the less said the better.

Johnson's favorite companion was a well-known prostitute named Belle Schreiber; he had another, named Etta Terry Duryea, also a white woman, who occupied a respectable station in life. Born twenty-eight years before in Hempstead, Long Island, and brought up in Brooklyn, Etta had been divorced from Clarence C. Duryea, an eastern racing man. Jack referred to Etta as "Mrs. Johnson," but continued to associate with Belle Schreiber; in spite of this Etta maintained the relationship, and it was eventually legitimized in marriage on January 18, 1911.

The search for a promoter continued. Jeffries' man Sam Berger had been talking with Tuxedo Ed Graney, who had staged a number of sporting events in California, then one of the few states where the law permitted "exhibition boxing bouts." Tuxedo Ed and his associate Jack Gleason proposed to raise money for a San Francisco stadium and to supply the gratuities for local officials and the press. Graney and Gleason knew their business, yet failed to convince Jeffries and Berger that they saw the full possibilities of the Johnson-Jeffries fight, which was to be called the Battle of the Century. Jim Jeffries believed that an unusual opportunity called for a unique entrepreneur, and so the choice remained in the air.

Then, out of Alaska came a man who seemed to meet every requirement that Jeffries demanded a fight promoter should have: his name was George Lewis Rickard. Respected as a gambler who always paid off, "Tex" Rickard travelled first class even when he was broke. Except for his metropolitan tailoring, he might have passed for the steely-eyed western movie star William S. Hart; he had acquired that same cold, level gaze as a faro dealer in the Klondike. Back in the United States now and looking for a sound proposition, Rickard talked to Jeffries and suggested that the fighters ask potential backers to bid for the match. He also interviewed Johnson, giving a journalist the chance to manufacture a tale that he poured out a shower of gold coins to dazzle Johnson into agreement. The truth is that Johnson was far from simple-minded and needed no tricks to catch his attention when Rickard sat down to talk. Rickard had the backing of Thomas Cole, a rich Minnesota mining engineer with whom he had done business in Alaska, and looked as good to Johnson as he did to Jeffries. Both principals agreed to come to New York to make a final selection among the possible promoters, naming December 1, 1909, as the day of decision.

Though public formalities still had to be attended to, Rickard was by now clearly in charge, and he carried off the signing ceremonies with his customary flair. In holding a meeting to discuss the fight in New York City, he would be breaking the law: even the planning of a fight to be held in another state was forbidden there. But Rickard wanted the coverage of the metropolitan press and thought the authorities might overlook the meeting, which was to be held on Broadway at the Albany Hotel. Then, on the day before the conference, word came that District Attorney William Travers Jerome had ordered his police to break up any meeting at which a prize fight was to be organized or announced. Rickard solved the difficulty by booking a private dining room at a German hotel across the river in Hoboken. He had already given the newspapermen their gratuities, and all that remained to be done was the ordering of cold meats, sandwiches, whiskey, champagne, and a tub of potato salad. Then as now, reporters numbered free food and drink among their natural rights.

In Hoboken, Tuxedo Ed Graney protested that Rickard had "horned in on the whole thing." Johnson said that so far as he was concerned, money had always done the talking. Jeffries seemed to be in a bad humor that was not helped by the clownish sight of Jack Gleason's overcoat, a tentlike garment that reached within an inch of the ground. Among others present was the politician Sunny Jim Coffroth of San Francisco, who was said to "control all boxing on the Pacific coast." Someone identified as "a man close to Rickard" passed the word that "Sunny Jim has been taken care of, and Gleason will be in on the deal, but Ed Graney is out in the cold." From their expressions in the news photographs, this would seem to have been an accurate statement. The fight was definitely scheduled for July 4, in San Francisco, and it became known that no opposition was expected from Governor James C. Gillett of California or San Francisco's Mayor Edward H. McCarthy.

In fact, everything was set. Rickard called for order, and one of his assistants opened the envelopes containing the bids. Apparently to no one's surprise, Sunny Jim pledged the fighters a purse of $51,000; Tuxedo Ed Graney offered $81,000; and Rickard's guarantee was $101,000, which he laid on the table in sight drafts on Thomas Cole's Minneapolis bank. Rickard was declared proprietor and promoter of the Battle of the Century, and as such his first act was to hand each fighter a bonus of $10,000 for signing the contracts that his lawyers placed before them. With this business concluded, the reporters hastened to the telephones, and then trampled elderly German waiters in a rush at the buffet tables, which they stripped with practiced voracity.

Out to the United States and the world went the news: Johnson and Jeffries were going to fight. Not included was a rumor that in addition to the bonus for each fighter, Rickard had paid $12,000 to settle a gambling debt incurred by Jeffries. Nor did the wire services carry any of the complicated rumors as to the "actual" deal between Jeffries and Johnson. Indeed, there was no deal, other than that Rickard's guarantee should be divided at sixty per cent for the winner, forty per cent for the loser. But what most mattered now in the public mind was that the "hopes of the white race," as one newspaper put it, would be carried "on the worthy shoulders of sturdy Jim Jeffries, undefeated champion of champions."

With their match settled, each of the fighters proceeded in his own manner. Jeffries returned to California to continue training and weight reducing under the direction of James J. Corbett and the famous wrestler Farmer Burns. There is evidence that he had been secretly training even before his trip to Carlsbad. In any event, he now settled down to it under the eyes of the press, and much material got into print about the solidity and strength of his arms and legs and the aggressiveness of his disposition. Johnson set out on a tour of the European music halls, performing an act which consisted of a few songs, a dance routine, a bit of playing on the bull fiddle, and a brief lecture on boxing. Etta accompanied him, along with a party of managers, valets, and secretaries; they spent Christmas of 1909 in London. On this expedition, Etta did something to earn her keep; in previous years she had shown talent in Brooklyn amateur theatricals, and she began to appear as part of Johnson's act. Thus they unconsciously tapped a deep vein of public emotion, by bringing to mind the folk tale of beauty and the beast.

Back in the United States, Johnson stopped in Chicago as the publicity for the big fight got under way and was arrested for speeding in his scarlet racing car at Twelfth Street and Michigan Avenue. Putting into Johnson's mouth the picturesque language reporters had invented for him, the Chicago *Inter-Ocean* had him saying, "Stand back, Mr. White Offisah, and let dem colored peoples hab a look at me." Unperturbed by the linguistic libel, and unrepentant after paying a fine, Johnson went to San Francisco the last week in May, 1910, to start his training for the Jeffries fight.

Meanwhile, reports from Jeffries' camp at Rowardennan in the northern part of California had it that "the

big fellow" was in a ferocious mood, that he ran fifteen miles a day, and that his sparring partners lived in fear of demolition. This propaganda was handed out by the former heavyweight champion, Jim Corbett, who was general manager, chief tactician, and director of psychological warfare for the Jeffries crowd. "Take it from me," he would say to the newspapermen, "the black boy has a yellow streak, and Jeff will bring it out when he gets him into that ring." Such training-camp dispatches soon got away from the sports departments and out on the front page, where they unrolled for column after column under headlines about "The White Man" and "The Giant Black." Thus, as July 4 drew nearer, a feeling of racial rivalry began to permeate the air; people were exposed to it as they took in their newspapers with the milk in the morning or read the headlines over a fellow passenger's shoulder coming home on the train.

Some educated Negroes did what they could to deflate the idea that Rickard's boxing show symbolized a struggle of race against race. The Reverend Reverdy C. Ransom of the Bethel African Methodist Church in New York City, for example, said, "No respectable colored minister in the United States is interested in the pugilistic contest between Johnson and Jeffries, from the standpoint of race. We do not think that Jack Johnson thinks or has ever thought of holding the championship for the 'black race.' Johnson is not trying to win the Negro championship, but to hold and defend his title against all comers, regardless of race or color."

Not all Negroes in the United States took Mr. Ransom's position, for many black people liked the idea of a symbolic champion as much as some of the whites found satisfaction in the same idea from the opposite racial point of view. The Chicago *Defender* was the first highly successful crusading newspaper founded by and for Negroes, and it accepted the theme that racial rivalry was implicit in the match between Johnson and Jeffries. Indeed, it hammered this one note as hard as Jeffries was supposed to be pounding his sparring mates. The *Defender* was worthy of attention: the paper had made a fortune for its publisher, Robert Sengstacke Abbott, who lived in a mansion, kept a box at the opera, carried a gold-headed cane, and wore a silk hat, long-tailed coat, striped trousers, and spats. Little of this dignity came through in the columns of the *Defender*, for Abbott believed in keeping his readers stirred up. His gift for sensationalism almost equalled that of William Randolph Hearst, as he showed in a cartoon which was printed on the front page of the *Defender* a few weeks before the fight. The picture had Jack shaking hands with Jeffries in the ring, with the front rows occupied by men exhibiting

a sign that read: "JIM CROW DELEGATES." The referee was a figure with the face of Satan, bearded and dressed as Uncle Sam, and labelled "Public Sentiment." He was saying to Jim Jeffries, "We're with you this time—go ahead." Ranged beside Jeffries were three menacing figures labelled "Race Hatred," "Prejudice," and "Negro Persecution." The legend above the cartoon was: "HE WILL HAVE THEM ALL TO BEAT," and below: "The future welfare of his people forms a part of the stake."

Meanwhile, in San Francisco, Rickard seemed to have found the ideal site for a big professional heavyweight boxing match. Local boosters had called the city the Paris of America, and though San Francisco may not have justified the sobriquet on cultural grounds, it was second to none in greedy hack drivers, exorbitant hotels, and unspeakable vices advertised and practiced in the resorts of the night-life area known as the Barbary Coast. But even in the Paris of America there were reformers, who made up for their small numbers by their earnestness and zeal. The moment the fight was announced they opened a campaign by letter, telegram, public meetings, and private interviews to get it stopped. Governor Gillett felt the heat and became uneasy. Hoping to please everybody, he announced that so far as he knew, the match was merely a "sparring contest," and he found nothing in the state law to forbid it. Needless to say, this merely increased the reformers' fury. Gillett had an exaggerated notion of his own importance and dreamed of Washington. It is therefore understandable that his anguish increased when a Mr. George Rockwell of Cincinnati brought into being "a national organization of business men and church people to prevent this outrage." Rockwell printed one million postcards addressed to Gillett with the message: "STOP THE FIGHT. THIS IS THE 20TH CENTURY." Thus the institution of professional boxing itself and not the color of Johnson's skin became the point of issue. Groaning in his mansion at Sacramento, Gillett cursed the day Tex Rickard came to California.

What pained Gillett was balm to Rickard, who heartily approved of the reformers, considering them so many unsalaried press agents for the fight. He continued preparations and built a yellow-pine arena to hold 25,000 spectators. Nevertheless, though Rickard was not aware of it, Gillett was beginning to cave in. There were signs and portents: one of the most startling was the spectacle of fifty ministers praying before the state capitol that the Governor would be moved to stop the fight. Rickard took this as gilt-edged publicity—that was the way *he* did things. Then one morning while he watched the driving of the last nails into the pine stadium, he received a private message that made him take seriously the thought of treachery in the Governor's mansion: even that wily politician Sunny Jim Coffroth was worried. He had reason to be, as Rickard soon found out, for heat from Washington was being felt in Sacramento.

The first hint of trouble had come to Sunny Jim from a spy in the office of the San Francisco Board of Trade. Its president, a respectable San Franciscan named William R. Wheeler, had received a telegram from Congressman William S. Bennett of New York, chairman of the House Committee on Foreign Affairs, stating that the "prospective fight" stood in the way of efforts to secure the Panama-Pacific Exposition of 1915 for San Francisco. This was very bad. While it was true that the Johnson-Jeffries match would bring from fifteen to twenty thousand visitors into town and would greatly increase business for the various institutions catering to the wants of tourists, that bonanza would continue only for a week at most; the exposition would last all summer. Governor Gillett knew that nothing must be allowed to jeopardize it, and after learning of the Bennett message, he called for his attorney general. "Go to San Francisco and tell Rickard to get out of my state," said Gillett. "Tell him to take Johnson and Jeffries with him. What he is planning is a prize fight, and against the law." Rickard received the order in a few hours; though forewarned, he was helpless. This was on the evening of June 15, less than three weeks before the

fight. Next morning the front page of every metropolitan paper in the country carried as its banner headline some variation of: "GILLETT VETOES THE BIG FIGHT." Rickard had the publicity of a lifetime—and no place to cash it in.

The circumstances under which Congressman Bennett had sent his telegram demonstrated the power of reform in that era: it showed, moreover, that the central strength of the movement lay in organized Protestantism. A good churchman, Bennett had gone as a lay delegate to the annual General Assembly of the Presbyterian Church in Atlantic City early in June. The consensus of the ministers and laymen at this highest gathering of Presbyterians was that all citizens and legislators be admonished to consider the evil of prize fighting and stamp it out. It was therefore obvious that, though not officially acting for his fellow Presbyterians, Mr. Bennett was reflecting their conviction when he used his influence to stop the San Francisco fight.

Mayor McCarthy of San Francisco was out of town when Gillett's announcement hit the front pages. Now he cut short an eastern trip and hurried back, pausing between trains in Chicago to say to reporters: "I am running San Francisco. I am taking no orders from Gillett or his attorney general. You can bet your last dollar the big fight will be pulled off in my town just as advertised." But he quieted down when he got home and heard about the danger of losing the Pan-American Exposition. As for James C. Gillett, he was lucky that Sacramento was not the Klondike. However, he had his reward. The *New York Times* editorialized, "Governor Gillett has assumed national stature. He deserves the heartiest praise of all good citizens." This praise was echoed in church and reform circles for the next few weeks, but Gillett sank into obscurity and was forgotten.

Those who thought expulsion from California meant cancellation of the fight were disappointed by Rickard's next move. Instead of giving in, he ordered the stadium dismantled and the timbers held in readiness for shipment to another location. Searching for a site within the United States, he called on Governor Denver S. Dickerson of Nevada, a man of broad views who ruled over a population of only 40,000 people, of whom a negligible number were ministers or women. Nevada was the only state in the union where prize fighting was not forbidden by law. Indeed, the state seemed to have few laws about anything, and was altogether a pleasant sort of place, with magnificent diamond-clear desert nights compensating for the heat of the days. When Rickard asked permission to hold the fight in the small but lively city of Reno, the Governor had only one question.

"Just tell me, man to man, it's on the level, Tex," said Dickerson. When assured that the bout would be honestly fought, the Governor gave his blessing; the promoter shipped the stadium timbers to Reno, and the boxers followed with their staffs of trainers, advisers, and jesters. It should be noted that Governor Dickerson's doubts about the honesty of the fight seemed not entirely baseless. On all sides the tale was told that Johnson had guaranteed a victory for Jeffries. "You heard nothing but fake, fix and double cross everywhere," wrote the foremost boxing expert of the day, Tad Dorgan. Partly because of the incessant rumor, Jeffries was a ten to seven favorite in the betting

when the boxers encamped near Reno. Few people asked why a fix would be necessary if Jeffries was so powerful he could kill a man with one blow. And no one tried to explain what advantage there could be for Johnson in such an arrangement. Johnson had in cash a $2,500 loan from Rickard plus his $10,000 bonus; even if he managed to get his training expenses entirely on credit, and so had this bankroll intact to bet on Jeffries—and getting the money down would be an extremely delicate transaction—the returns at the quoted odds would be less than $9,000. But the winner's end of the purse would be $60,600, and if Johnson bet his roll on himself to win, and beat Jeffries, there would be around $17,000 more. So it was clear that someone would have to find a great deal of money to buy Johnson off. Moreover, it would have to be assumed that Jack had no pride—an assumption not justified by the facts of his fighting career: pride, indeed, was the power of his life.

It should be borne in mind, however, that amid the babble about fixes, frames, and yellow streaks there were men of judgment and discrimination. Governor Dickerson was one of these, and he went to Johnson's camp at The Willows, a roadhouse four miles outside Reno, to have an unbiassed look at what was going on. Wearing a wide-brimmed Panama hat, the Governor bowed in courtly fashion when presented to Belle Schreiber and looked on with interest as Johnson boxed with the gigantic Al Kaufman, once an opponent and now a training partner. The newspapers reported that the Governor remained calm when Jack "drew the claret" in "tapping Kaufman on the beak." The next sparring partner was George Cotton, who "drew the ruby" by cutting Johnson's lip. Jack's return was so rapid that Dickerson did not see the movement of his arm; Cotton's knees gave way, and he held himself up by the ropes. Johnson stepped back, Cotton left the ring semiconscious, and Johnson's manager, Sig Hart, threw a bucket of water over his head to bring him around.

"What happened to him there?" asked Dickerson.

A reporter answered, "Johnson hit him on the jaw with his left and almost put him out."

"Put him out of where?"

"Quit your kidding, Governor," said the reporter. "You know what I mean. He was nearly knocked out."

"Oh, I see," said Dickerson.

"Didn't you ever see a fight before?"

"Lots of 'em, but not like this. The others were with guns, where men sank to their death. In this affair, no one seems to suffer much hurt."

Though disappointed at the lack of fatalities, Governor Dickerson called the reporters together at the conclusion of his visit and announced, "I have never seen a man who can whip Jack Johnson as he stands today, and I am forced to bet on him."

The Governor was too sensible to issue such a statement without having first seen Jeffries; but this made no impression on the thousands of bettors throughout the country who were putting their money on "Big Jim." Nor did Dickerson's estimate have any effect on the experts who were now beginning to flock into Reno. It was turned aside, for example, by the elderly and famous trainer and physical culturist William Muldoon, who was later to be New York State Boxing Commissioner and who possessed such immense rectitude that he was called "the Old Roman." Muldoon faced an attentive half-circle of reporters in front of his hotel and said, "The Negro won't fight. I pick Jeffries."

Equally sure of the outcome was Jack London. He arrived in the town accompanied by two tramps called Watertank Willie and Seattle Sam; the author's face was swollen with bruises he had sustained in a fight with a bartender at Ogden, Utah. London at once began to load the wires with copy and generally to take himself with the intense seriousness that seems to overcome literary men amid the aura of importance and significance surrounding a heavyweight championship fight.

London's first dispatch had hardly cleared the wires before the renowned old ex-champion John L. Sullivan arrived on the scene. He was there on Rickard's invitation as the elder statesman of boxing and was also under contract to report the fight for the *New York Times*. Sullivan had not touched liquor for five years; he had grown immensely fat and wore a little gray cap that made him look like Tweedledum or his twin as he waddled down the main street of Reno. Sullivan's first statement was, "It looks like a frame-up."

When Sullivan's remark reached Jeffries' training quarters at a roadhouse called Moana Springs, on the Truckee River, he was so annoyed that he cried, "That big stiff better not come here or I'll turn the fire hose on him! I always hated a knocker!"

The atmosphere of Jeffries' camp was unhappy. The staff had grown: the Olympic trainer Mike Murphy had joined as physical director, while Eddie Leonard ("the Minstrel Man") and Walter C. Kelly were in attendance as entertainers. In time, Kelly was to become the uncle of the future Princess Grace of Monaco, but at the moment he was known for a vaudeville act called "The Virginia Judge," which drew its humor from the supposed combination of craftiness and stupidity displayed by Negroes before the bar of justice. Side by side with Leonard, Kelly could put on a show that would fill a Broadway theatre, but at the Jeffries

camp the comedians worked in vain. Jim was in such a bad mood that not even the administering of a Mickey Finn to one of the camp servants could bring a smile to his drawn face. Nor could the wonders of nature divert him: he remained morose at the sight of Halley's comet sparkling across the Nevada skies. "I told you not to wake me up to see no comet!" Jeffries cried. "Who cares about comets? I want my sleep!"

While Jeffries continued to fret, Johnson worked hard. His evenings, however, were all gaiety and relaxation. Jack liked the desert sunsets, and he would stand outside the roadhouse watching the blue sky turn to amethyst and rose. Cool air drifted from the mountains; he would hear the mechanical piano in the taproom strike up "Oh, You Beautiful Doll" and see the glow of oil lamps at the windows. It was time to go inside, get out the bull fiddle, and cut a few capers. Two volunteer masters of ceremonies were usually present at these festivities in the persons of the wine agents Bob Vernon and Harry Lehr.* As the late afternoon sky began to deepen, Vernon and Lehr would drive out to The Willows at the head of a train of automobiles loaded with eastern society women and hampers of champagne; Japanese butlers accompanied the two salesmen and opened the plentiful bottles, pouring and serving the wine. The fashionable women had not come to Reno to see the fight, but to obtain divorces under the Nevada six weeks' residence law. Sometimes they caught a glimpse of Belle Schreiber; on the last day of June, Belle went to San Francisco, and Etta Duryea appeared. Like Belle, she stayed in the background, and reporters confused the two women, referring to each of them, on occasion, as "Johnson's white wife."

* Lehr was also the social consultant to Mrs. Stuyvesant Fish of New York City.

In spite of the merriment in the taproom, The Willows was an armed camp. Johnson owned several pistols, keeping one in his pocket and the others near his bedside. Each night, after the mechanical piano was stilled and the last car had rolled away to Reno, a sentry paced beneath the windows of the house. He was a dependable man named Cal McVey, an old-time National League catcher, and he carried a shotgun. Perhaps these precautions were excessive, but like everyone else, Johnson was reading the papers with their stories of fixes and frames and unidentifiable figures lurking in the background. More practically, however, he was afraid of a robbery. Some of the ablest thieves in the United States had come to Reno, or were on their way. The eminent bank robber Cincinnati Slim was already there, and the bandit known as the Sundance Kid, later to be shot to pieces in South America, was expected any day. Also walking the streets of Reno were such celebrities of terror as Won Let, the hatchet man for the New York branch of the Hip Sing Tong, who was known to have dispatched between twenty and thirty fellow Chinamen. And in the same newspapers that poured out column after column about the training, the gathering crowds, and the betting rumors, there were items about Jack's money and jewelry, which any reasonably alert jewel thief would surely have noted; Johnson took pains to make it known that Cal McVey was on hand.

Reno came to a boil in the final week preceding the Fourth of July. Rickard had the timbers from the San Francisco arena in town at midnight of June 27; before dawn, carpenters were working by torchlight. They were to get premium pay, but inspiring them even more than the extra money was the meeting of an emergency, the paving of the way for a great event. To the public, Reno became for the next seven days the hub of the universe. Thinking it over when he had

become a veteran editor, Henry Wales of the Chicago *Tribune* wrote that no event in modern times so permeated the mind of the world until Charles Lindbergh's flight from Long Island to Paris seventeen years later. And no event, said Wales, had attracted so many reporters; by his count more than three hundred were at work in Reno by the end of June. At the time, newspaper pages were broad and deep and set in small type except for the headlines. Reporters therefore had to write long stories, and those at Reno made their editors happy by sending out around one million words a day. What this coverage would have amounted to with radio and television added is beyond estimate.

That final week in Reno may have been the last stand of uninhibited American masculinity; undoubtedly it was the last great convention of men who carried the title of "sport." The term described a man who was an amateur or semiprofessional gambler and therefore a student of form and odds, a man of wide and easy views, tolerant, willing to live and let live—most probably something of a dandy according to his means and background—in short, a Corinthian, a blood. In his highest form he could be called a sportsman. The ordinary sport of the big cities and his brother of the small towns could be anybody from a barber in Kokomo to Harry Payne Whitney of New York, who booked four private cars to take a party of "Wall Street men" to Reno; the sport could be a tobacconist in Petoskey or he could be the old Yale halfback Tom Shevlin, who arrived in Reno wearing a dove-gray waistcoat and a straw hat with a club ribbon and took Johnson for a run in his racing car. If a sport could by any imaginable means get free of his women and put his hands on ticket money, with a stake for drink, wagers, and shelter, then some time toward the end of June he was up and away and heading for Reno in the Great American Desert.

There the sports of whatever degree found a city of little more than ten thousand trying to take care of some seventeen thousand visitors. Not even a pool table could be rented for sleeping purposes and every private house that accepted paying guests was full to overflowing. Hundreds of the sports, to be sure, had come in special trains and lived in the Pullman cars lined up on the spur tracks of the Southern Pacific at a junction three miles south of town. Other hundreds arrived in honking, dusty automobiles carrying signs that read: "Reno or Bust!" and slept in these vehicles. Some slept on the floors of saloons, and others by all accounts did not sleep at all. For their accommodation, the gambling houses employed croupiers in shifts, so that the blackjack layouts, roulette wheels, and bird cages in which dice were mechanically thrown kept going night and day. In these places men crowded four deep around the tables. The proprietors expected them to bet substantial money; as the Chicago *Daily News* put it, "the two-bit man is not wanted in Reno today." A Colonel Horatio Byrne stated that "you will see the solidest type of man at the ringside. Nowadays the cheap man can't afford to patronize the pugilistic game with any ostentation. It takes money to see a big fight right." Jim Corbett's brother Tom, who called himself official bookie for the match, said, "Three million dollars will change hands on the outcome of this fight."

Another source of profit in the great gathering at Reno was in the robbing of the careless and often drunken sports who were easily identifiable among the crowds of Indians, cowboys, Mexicans, and miners on the streets. There were two elements among the professional thieves at Reno. The better class were the pickpockets, who worked in pairs known as the wire and the screen. The latter screened the victim's eyes with a newspaper, or otherwise distracted his attention, while the wire lifted his purse or watch. Even as a victim, the two-bit man met with scorn: more than one observer reported seeing scores of nickel-plated watches in the gutters of Reno, where thieves had thrown them in disgust on recognizing their low value. In the large cities, pickpockets were respected as skilled craftsmen by the police and often lived in amity with them. In Reno, however, Governor Dickerson held that the state's honor was involved and ordered all known pickpockets to be chased out of town on recognition or instantly jailed if caught with the goods.

The other class of thief, socially inferior to the pickpocket, was the lush-roller, who followed drinking men and robbed them when they collapsed. He would sometimes help induce collapse with a blackjack, and was despised by all bartenders, sports, and policemen as a human jackal. Against these predators, Dickerson assembled a strong force of deputized citizens, together with detectives from New York, Philadelphia, Chicago, Denver, and San Francisco; a detachment of Nevada State Rangers; and a patrol of Arizona Rangers, headed by their celebrated commander, Captain Cox. Even the bandits and vacationing bank robbers hesitated to cross Cox's path, for fear he might go into the dreaded gunfighter's crouch and draw one or both of the pistols that hung at his belt. But in spite of the guardians provided by Dickerson and the Reno Chamber of Commerce, many of the sports had unfortunate experiences, such as being robbed, cheated, sickened by bad liquor, or given diseases in the brothels.

The majority of the visitors, of course, knew their way about, and understood that losing money in gam-

bling houses was entertainment rather than speculation. An example of a sport who would be hard to swindle was Colonel Abe Slupsky, a St. Louis politician who arrived in his home city after the fight with three thousand dollars under porous plaster on his chest. "It was the only way to carry money in Reno," said the Colonel. "I would have stuck it on my back except there wasn't anybody I could trust to do it for me. The night before the fight, I kicked away twenty empty pocketbooks on the plank walks. The dips would take out the money and throw them away. The streets were full of them."

By now Johnson was in a state of euphoria. In the evenings, on his big fiddle, he plucked a rhythmical background for "I've Got Rings on My Fingers," "By the Light of the Silvery Moon," and "I Love My Wife, But Oh, You Kid." He clowned for the reporters and obliged them by falling in with the traditional vein of melon-devouring, chicken-stealing humor that was regarded as appropriate to his color.

"No stolen chicken ever passes the portals of my face," Johnson would say, pointing to his gold-filled teeth. "Chickens see the gleam in my eye and keep out of my way. Chicken and corn fritters are affinities. They are meant for each other and both are meant for me."

Jocosities of this sort lent credence to the rumors, now rising to their climax, that Johnson did not take the fight seriously; and in some quarters, such comedy was interpreted as meaning that Johnson had gorged himself out of shape to insure victory for Jeffries. A newspaper writer named W. P. McCloughlin went farther. First he posed the question, "Is Johnson a typical example of his race in the lack of that intangible 'something' that we call 'heart'?" McCloughlin thought Johnson had a great need of that intangible something, for he had "observed closely Jack's 'impenetrable guard'" and could not "see any reason why it is so designated." However, in "James Jeffries, the hope of the white race," he discerned "a gradually growing sullen ferocity." It might be supposed that Johnson was in danger if one also believed that this ferocity had at its service the most powerful physique in America. Indeed, the study of Jeffries' body in the training ring had inspired many a burst of purple writing, and the following sentence in a dispatch to the Chicago *Inter-Ocean* was regarded as worthy of Oscar Wilde: "Under his skin of bronze the muscles rippled like the placid surface of a body of water touched by a gentle breeze."

When Jeffries read this passage, he said it made him sick. Indeed, the more the writers extolled his size and strength, the deeper grew his melancholia. He was by now so dispirited that when Corbett brought John L. Sullivan out to Moana Springs, Jeffries not only failed to turn the fire hose on him, but shook his hand, and said, "I know you didn't mean what you said about me, John." Then he asked Sullivan how he should fight Johnson, and before the old champion could reply, went on to remark, "I don't see why I have to be the favorite." Sullivan looked him over carefully and said, "Jim, all I know is God Almighty hates a quitter."

As the time before the fight grew shorter, there came

another indication that betting on Jeffries would be throwing money away, and now it was William Muldoon who uttered the caveat. He visited the camp at Moana Springs and returned to the center of town to announce that "Jeffries' judgment of distance and timing is not what it should be. He will take punishment." And finally, those who were skeptical about Jeffries saw their doubts expressed on July 1 by a cartoon on the front page of the Chicago *Daily News*. The picture showed Johnson in ring clothes strumming on a bass fiddle that was labelled "Jeff." The caption beneath

read: "Hush, hush, don' yo' talk so loud!"

Three days later, on the morning of July 4, 1910, Jack Johnson got up early. For breakfast he ate four lamb cutlets, three scrambled eggs, and several slices of rare steak. Jeffries took only a little fruit, toast, and tea, but each man issued a statement in hearty style. Jeffries' manifesto was,

When the gloves are knotted on my hands and I stand ready to defend what is really my title, it will be at the request of the public, which forced me out of retirement. I realize full well just what depends on me, and I am not going to disappoint the public. That portion of the white race that has been looking to me to defend its athletic superiority may feel assured that I am fit to do my very best. If Johnson defeats me, I will shake his hand and declare him the greatest fighter the sporting world has ever known.

Johnson told the public,

Every fighter on the eve of his fight declares that he hopes the best man wins. I am quite sincere when I say that I do, and if Mr. Jeffries knocks me out or gains a decision over me, I will go into his corner and congratulate him as soon as I am able. My congratulations will not be fake. I mean it. Let me say in conclusion that I believe the meeting between Mr. Jeffries and myself will be a test of strength, skill, and endurance. I plan to gradually beat him down and finally make him take the count. However, should I meet defeat I will have no excuse to offer and will proclaim Mr. Jeffries king of them all.

This mood of statesmanlike tact was missing in the office of the Chicago *Defender*, where Robert S. Abbott pounded his typewriter in a frenzy. "If Johnson is forced to fight Jim Crow Delegations, race prejudice and insane public sentiment," Abbott wrote, "and if he wins in the face of all this, he is truly entitled to a Carnegie Hero Medal." There was no doubt in Abbott's mind as to the outcome of the fight, and he went on, "When the smoke of the battle clears away, and when the din of mingled cheers and groans have died away in the atmosphere, there will be deep mourning throughout the domains of Uncle Sam over Jeffries' inability to return the pugilistic sceptre to the Caucasian race." The pastor of St. Mark's African Methodist Episcopal Church, near Abbott's office, felt no such certainty about the result of the match. To help Johnson win, the minister opened the sanctuary early on Fourth of July morning for a prayer service that continued through the time the men were fighting at Reno. And numerous other Negro congregations all over the country did the same.

One of the most discerning reporters at the center of the nationwide web of excitement, emotion, and prayer was Arthur Ruhl, representing *Collier's* magazine. Sensitive to the surroundings as well as to the fight itself, he described the scene on the early afternoon of July 4, 1910, after the crowd was seated, and just before the fighters made their entrance:

You must imagine a bright green little oasis, ten or fifteen miles across, set in a sort of dish of bare enclosing mountains —brown mountains with patches of yellow and olive-green and exquisite veils of mauve and amethyst, and at their tops, blazing white in the clear air, patches of austere snow. In the center of all this a great pine bear-pit had been raised, glaring white and hot in the blazing desert sun, and into this at 1:30 o'clock that afternoon 20,000 men were crowded with their eyes fixed on a little roped square in the center.

The betting was 10 to 6 on Jeffries and the talk about 1,000 to 1. You couldn't hurt him—Fitzsimmons had landed enough times to kill an ordinary man in the first few rounds, and Jeffries had only shaken his head like a bull and bored in. The Negro might be a clever boxer, but he had never been up against a real fighter before. He had a yellow streak, there was nothing to it, and anyway, "Let's hope he kills the coon."

"That was about the mental atmosphere as Johnson, wrapped in a dressing gown and smiling his half-puzzled, rather pleading smile, climbed into the ring," Ruhl reported. Then, accompanied by Corbett and other trainers, Jim Jeffries strode down the aisle. Ruhl continued:

I had a seat directly opposite him, and I can unhesitatingly state that I have never seen a human being more calculated to strike terror into an opponent's heart than this scowling brown Colossus as he came through the ropes, stamped like a bull pawing the ground before his charge, and, chewing gum rapidly, glared at the black man across the ring. If looks could have throttled, burned, and torn to pieces, Mr. Jack Arthur Johnson would have disappeared that minute into a few specks of inanimate dust. The Negro had his back turned at the moment, and as he took his corner and his trainer and his seconds, crowding in front of him, concealed the white man, a sort of hoot, wolfish and rather terrible, went up from the crowd. "He daresen't look at him! *O-o-o!* Don't let him see him! Don't let him see him!" And when Jeffries pulled off his clothes with a vicious jerk, and standing erect and throwing out his chest, jabbed his great arms above his head once or twice, I don't suppose that one man in a hundred in that crowd would have given two cents for the Negro's chances.

Jim Corbett, however, was not looking at his man Jeffries. He had neglected making a visit to the enemy camp, depending for information on faulty intelligence of the gin-and-watermelon school, and as Corbett now got his first glimpse of Johnson, a terrible fear assailed him. He knew condition: Jack had not acquired that flat stomach leaning against a bar. "Jeff will find his yellow streak now," Corbett muttered to Farmer Burns. He did not need to add that if they had been mistaken about that streak, they were in for trouble.

Arthur Ruhl had overestimated the crowd; counting the journalists and politicians who came in on free

tickets, there were just over sixteen thousand people in the arena. As a special attention, Rickard had installed curtained boxes for the women getting divorces, who for the first time constituted a noticeable group of females at a prize fight.

Students of this affair should bear in mind that although women were present, many of the spectators were drunk, and others were enduring hangovers in dreadful heat that was retained and magnified in the wooden arena. Well might they shift on the resinous planks as Uncle Billy Jordan, the portly master of ceremonies, called up Sullivan, Corbett, Tommy Burns, Fitzsimmons, Tom Sharkey, Battling Nelson, and Abe Attel for perfunctory applause. Jordan endured the blast of heat in a high-crowned derby, watch-chained waistcoat, claw-hammer coat, and gates-ajar starched collar. At last the celebrities took their final bows, and Jordan yielded to Rickard, who, protecting his head from the sun by a hard straw hat and taking off his coat to reveal a pair of silk suspenders, prepared to referee the Battle of the Century—forty-five rounds for the championship of the world.

Rickard signalled for the opening gong. Outweighing Johnson by about twenty pounds, Jeffries advanced from his corner, and Jack came to meet him with his characteristic shuffling gait. Jeffries in his crouching style immediately took the fight to Johnson, and Jack worked with extreme caution in avoiding these opening rushes. His face was impassive, and his movements so economical that only an expert and unprejudiced eye could appreciate their smoothness and speed. As for Jeffries, for all his crouching, rushing, and swinging, there was no continuity to his attack, yet the crowd cheered him at the end of the round. Most of the spectators believed Jeffries was going to pin Johnson in a corner and beat down his defense by main strength and that everybody would then go home happy and rich. There was a comfortable murmur throughout the arena, like that of a concert audience settling down, after preliminary selections, for the main symphonic work.

The second round was much the same, Jeffries trying to reach Jack by means of a straight left, but doing no damage. Johnson still looked solemn and thoughtful, with the expression of one who is listening to sad news or attending a funeral. The sports took this as evidence of fear—and did not know what to think when in the middle of the next round Johnson suddenly flicked out his left glove in a jab that brought the crouching Jeffries up straight as though he had run into the edge of an open door. Now it was seen that Johnson was smiling and talking to Jeffries. Corbett heard him say, "Come on now, Mr. Jeff. Let me see what you got. *Do* something, man. This is for the cham-*peen-ship*." There was less rejoicing in the audience when this third round ended, but they were more puzzled than alarmed.

In the fourth round, Johnson took the offensive, and kept the left jab flickering in Jeffries' face. "I can go on like this all afternoon, Mr. Jeff," Johnson taunted. At the opening of the seventh round, Jack shuffled out with such deceptive quickness that he was able to land a stupefying right cross to the jaw before Jeffries' hands were in position. From this point on, anyone who knew about fighting could see that unless Johnson left himself open to a lucky blow, Jeffries had no chance. Boxing wildly, visibly slowing down, the former champion managed to last the round, then collapsed on his stool with his right eye closing, his face marked and swollen. He endured more pounding in the eighth round. In the ninth, he tried desperately to take the initiative again, but he hit only elbows and gloves.

To the horror of the crowd, Jeffries had lost his breath by the end of the twelfth round; he was still struggling to get air into his lungs when the bell brought the men out for the thirteenth. There were scattered cries of "Stop it! Don't let him be knocked out!"—but Rickard allowed the fight to go on, and Johnson kept smashing away with left and right. By the final seconds of the fourteenth round, Jeffries was in such distress that he could barely raise his arms. In the fifteenth, Jack knocked Jeffries half out of the ring; friends pushed him back, Rickard ignoring this violation of the rules, and Johnson chopped him down again with a left to the head. Somehow Jeffries got on his feet, to receive three snapping blows to the face that knocked him back to the floor. Sam Berger threw in a towel to concede defeat, but Rickard did not see it, and counted ten over the inert Jeffries. Then Rickard lifted the fist of Jack Johnson as indisputable heavyweight champion of the world.

A few seconds later, at the Pekin Theatre on Chi-

cago's South Side, where 1,500 Negroes gathered to receive bulletins of the fight, a man holding a slip of paper ran on the stage. The master of ceremonies took the paper, glanced at it, raised himself on his toes and filled his lungs. With arms extended he bellowed, "Johnson wins!" It seemed as if the roof fell in; then the members of the audience rushed for the street, climbing each other's backs in the doorways. Into State Street they poured to join thousands of other Negroes, who were capering, shouting, and beating on dishpans, while over it all the continuous thundering of extra-large firecrackers made a sound like a great battle. Across the country similar parades were forming, principally in Negro neighborhoods, but sometimes on white territory as well. At first, white persons viewing the Negro demonstrations took no action, and some applauded the celebrators, though probably with ironic intent. The trouble would come with darkness when the liquor got to work.

As night came on frolic turned into riot, and riot into civil war, small in scale but deadly in result, in both North and South. Exulting Negroes clashed with frightened or resentful whites, and by morning reports of death and injury had come from towns and cities in Pennsylvania, Maryland, Ohio, Mississippi, Virginia, Missouri, Georgia, Arkansas, and Colorado. There had been a gun battle at Uvaldia, Georgia, leaving three Negroes dead and scores of whites and Negroes wounded. This was the worst rioting of the night, but throughout the country there were eight other deaths that could be directly charged to the racial friction arising from Johnson's victory and Jeffries' defeat. In the New York metropolitan area, Irish hoodlums as well as Negro rowdies welcomed the chance to make trouble. A typical uproar took place in Brooklyn when three Irish toughs heard a Negro named Edward Coleman say to a dog, "Lie down there, Jeffries."

"You have your nerve to call that dog Jeffries," said John Dermody. "Why don't you call it Johnson?"

"Because Johnson is black and this dog is yellow," the Negro answered. Then the fight started, but it was not one-sided, as Coleman had friends nearby.

In Muskogee, Oklahoma, a man who claimed to be a second cousin of John L. Sullivan attacked two Negroes with a knife but was seized by the police before he could do any damage. There was rioting in Pittsburgh, Philadelphia, Baltimore, Wilmington, and Norfolk, resulting in many injuries and hundreds of arrests; the entire town of Keystone, West Virginia, was in the control of a Negro mob until late in the afternoon of July 5. All told, two white persons and nine Negroes met death, the Negro victims including two killed by their own people. Observing these lamentable events across the gap of more than fifty years, it is possible to theorize that the trouble did not come so much from the undeniable circumstance that Johnson was champion, as from the glorying over whites in which the blacks, perhaps understandably, indulged.

At Reno, the series of happenings that triggered the rioting had come to a confused end. As Rickard dropped his arm, Johnson said to Sig Hart, "I think I'll give one glove to Corbett and one to Jeff." But Corbett hurried Jeffries

away without waiting for any gestures from Johnson. With his closed eye, bloody and swollen face, and fumbling movements, Jeffries looked like the loser he was. Corbett and Farmer Burns helped him from the ring; then he pulled himself together and stalked away. One has the feeling that Jeffries was entitled to some recognition of his gameness; but his performance had been so poor, and his defeat such a disappointment—and to many, such an unpleasant surprise—that there were no cheers to warm his heart as he left the arena.

But the situation held at least enough tension to start some long-lived rumors. One still generally believed today has it that Sig Hart hustled Jack out of the arena to an automobile and drove a fast fifty miles into the desert to a special train waiting at a lonely stop. The fact is that Johnson walked out unmolested and went to The Willows, where he put on a blue silk suit and a crimson bow tie. Etta had watched the

fight from one of Rickard's box seats for ladies; she now changed her costume, putting on a fresh pongee dress and picture hat, and joined Jack for a ride through the center of Reno in the back seat of an open touring car. Johnson appeared to be in no danger, and the crowd was apathetic. It seemed that those who had an emotional as well as financial investment in Jeffries were still in shock. Indeed, when Jack's car halted in the crowd on the street in front of the Golden Hotel, many persons came up and shook his hand. He left Reno at 9:50 P.M. in a special car attached to a train bound for Chicago. The car was fitted with a buffet, phonograph, and piano; Jack was happy and chatted genially with Hart and others. He was observed to be consuming "his share of the champagne" but not to be drunk. Over the desert sped the car, its lighted windows passing with a jangle of ragtime and a swirl of dust that settled under the stars.

Jim Jeffries also was riding in a private car, but heading in the opposite direction, for San Francisco. He was attended by his wife, Berger, Farmer Burns, Corbett, and several reporters. Morose and melancholy, Jeffries took no liquor; surprisingly, he spoke with frankness to the newspapermen. "I could never have whipped Jack Johnson at my best," the former champion said. "I couldn't have hit him. No, I couldn't have reached him in a thousand years."

This time Jim Jeffries' retirement was permanent; he returned to his farm in California, and there he lived to a prosperous old age. The victorious Jack Johnson was hardly so fortunate. The years that followed were more notable for his misadventures with the law than for his exploits in the ring. Women were his undoing. In September, 1912, Etta Terry Duryea Johnson shot herself at his Chicago cabaret, the Café de Champion; she was in her grave scarcely two months when he married another white girl, Lucille Cameron. The next spring Johnson was charged with and convicted of violating the Mann Act (that is, transporting a woman across a state line for immoral purposes), largely on the testimony of his old friend Belle Schreiber. He promptly fled the country, one step ahead of his jailers. Two years later, on April 5, 1915, Jack Johnson finally lost his title. In a bout held in Havana, he was floored after twenty-six rounds by an-

other "white hope," the 250-pound giant, Jess Willard.

Not until 1920 did the first black champion end his exile, surrendering himself to federal authorities at the Mexican border; he served a year and a day at Leavenworth—where, ironically, the warden was the former governor of Nevada, Denver S. Dickerson. For the rest of his life, Johnson made a shabby and unspectacular living from carnival side shows, vaudeville, and an occasional fight. In 1945, when another great Negro boxer, Joe Louis, held the heavyweight title, Jack Johnson fought his last exhibition; he was then sixty-eight years old. That April he died in an automobile accident: to the very end he never lost his penchant for fast cars. At the funeral in Chicago, a minister of his race delivered what may well have been Johnson's truest epitaph: "Jack struck a double blow when he became heavyweight champion. If we hadn't had a Jack, we wouldn't have a Joe now."
—The Editors

on foot; but the half-wild range cattle could be handled only by skilled *vaqueros* mounted on fleet, well-trained horses. Spain, in her colonial regulations, had decreed that no Indian should be permitted to own or ride a horse. Thus all the arduous work of handling the range cattle and range horses devolved on the Spanish men.

Each *vaquero* needed a riding string of twelve to fifteen horses to handle his job properly. These animals were not shod, and seldom tasted grain. A *vaquero*'s mount needed several days of rest after each day of work, to regain his strength and to allow his hoofs to grow. Each Spanish family also needed several horses for transportation, for there were no carriage roads on the frontier. Many additional horses were needed for military patrols, and for exploring expeditions or the pursuit of raiding Indians. A large herd of breeding stock was necessary to supply all these animals.

The care of these thousands of horses required a good deal of menial labor, furnished, of course, by the Indians. Indian boys brought fresh horses in for their masters to use, and returned the tired ones to the corrals. They did the saddling, unsaddling, and rubbing down. They fed and watered the animals, and cleaned the stables and corrals. Sometimes a rancher, careless of the regulations forbidding an Indian to ride, would send a boy to help drive in a herd from the hills; sometimes, leaving on an extended journey, he would choose two or three Indians to ride with him —to look after the spare mounts and to handle the camp chores. In the face of emergencies the decrees of King Philip of Spain carried little weight on the frontier, far from the eyes of the nearest government official. So, in one way or another, the stable boys learned how to ride and how to handle horses.

Most of the Pueblo Indians resigned themselves to servitude under the Spanish. They had no place to run, no place to hide. But for a stable boy there was one avenue of escape if conditions became too harsh or masters too domineering; and his work with the horses seemed to breed in him more spirit than showed in the field hand. By watching for a favorable opportunity, the stable boy could slip away some dark evening with two or three of the best horses, and be off to an independent tribe, safe from effective pursuit. He might risk death or further enslavement, but there was always a good chance that the tribe would accept him and his horses. Then he could teach them the art of horsemanship, and could help his hosts secure more horses from the ranches.

With such a teacher, and some tame, well-trained

horses to work with, the wild tribe could rapidly learn how to use this wonderful new mode of transport. Soon they would want more horses and would take their goods off to trade with the Spanish, as they had been doing for years. But the Spanish were reluctant to trade horses to the Indians: such trading took place in towns, under the eyes of Spanish colonial officials.

When the Spanish refused to exchange horses for dried meat and tanned robes, the Indians sought other articles of trade, and found one so valuable to the Spanish that the laws would be suspended in special cases. The Indians traded men.

The Spanish, in an effort to discourage the escape of Pueblo Indians, offered cloth and weapons for any runaways the wild tribes could capture. But the Indians soon learned that the Spanish would pay higher prices for mission Indians, and still higher prices to ransom Spaniards captured by the tribes. They demanded horses for such captives, and the priests argued with the civil authorities that it was better to bend the law a little than to leave Christians in heathen hands.

Thus, year by year, the tribes adjacent to the Spanish settlements learned to use horses, and slowly increased their herds. The first documentary evidence of the use of horses by Indians in the American West comes sixty-one years after the arrival of Oñate's colony: In 1659 the governor at Sante Fe sent to Mexico City an official report of a raid from the northwest by a band of mounted Navaho Apaches.

Finally, in 1680, the Pueblo Indians rose up against their masters. They resented the brutal treatment, the forced labor, and, above all, the strict laws against their ancient religious ceremonies. A deposed medicine man, Popé, organized a widespread revolt, and on the appointed day the Pueblos attacked at many points in northern New Mexico, killing over 400 Spanish in the first attack. The 2,500 survivors withdrew to El Paso to wait for reinforcements from Mexico; but they had lost their homes, their farms, and all their herds to the Indians (see "Revolt in the Pueblos," by Alvin M. Josephy, Jr., in the June, 1961, AMERICAN HERITAGE).

The Pueblo Indians found the horse herds an embarrassment of riches. They were hard to manage on the range, and they ate the grass needed for sheep. Moreover, the Pueblos had no use for as many horses as the Spanish had abandoned. They were willing to trade large numbers of them to the Plains tribes to the northeast, and to the Navahos and Utes to the

W. M. Cary's Indian Boys Breaking a Pony *suggests that the breaking, while lots of fun, must sometimes have been mutual.*

northwest. The Pueblos also lacked the organization to patrol the ranges as the Spanish had done, and lost more horses to enemy raiders.

All through the Plains regions each band had friendly trade relations with two or three of its neighbors. A farming village would customarily trade with a hunting band to the south and another to the north. Each of these hunting bands in turn would trade with another farming village, the hunters in each case offering dried meat and buffalo robes for corn and squash. This helps to explain the rapid spread of horses to all the Plains tribes. The result was a basic pattern of horse culture, borrowed from the Spanish and common to all the western tribes using horses.

Typically, this trading pattern would provide each tribe at first with a few older, gentler horses. Nez Percé tradition, handed down by word of mouth to early white frontiersmen, gives an account of such an event. According to this story they got their first animal, a gentle white mare, from the Shoshone in the Boise Valley. Day after day the curious Nez Percés gathered from all around to watch the mare crop grass near the village. They learned how a horse acted: how it fed, how it exercised, how it rested. In a few weeks the mare dropped a foal, and the crowds increased.

Soon other villages sent south for horses of their own, to be treasured as curiosities and pets. At The Dalles, Oregon, some two hundred miles down river from the Nez Percé, the first few horses were led around at festivals and were shown at the big dances. Later they were used as pack animals, and finally as riding horses.

Although details of the first contacts with horses among the Plains tribes have been lost, they must have followed the Nez Percé pattern. In each case it would take a tribe only about ten to fifteen years to learn how to use the great innovation, and to build up a substantial herd.

Horses made life far easier, richer, and more exciting for the Plains tribes. One good horseman in a morning hunt could kill enough buffalo to supply his family with meat for weeks, and robes for a year. Now tepees could be much larger, for a horse could carry a lodge-covering weighing 200 to 300 pounds, and drag the many long tepee poles needed to support it. The whole band now had more leisure time, and more chance to develop the special Plains culture which was in full flower by 1800.

As for the impact of the horse on Indian warfare, it would be difficult to exaggerate. With the tremendous increase in mobility and speed, the Plains warrior became a truly formidable foe. General Randolph B. Marcy, a Regular Army officer with many years of experience in the West, wrote this impression of the mounted Indian in his memoirs:

His only ambition consists in being able to cope successfully with his enemy in war and in managing his steed with unfailing adroitness. He is in the saddle from boyhood to old age, and his favorite horse is his constant companion. It is when mounted that the prairie warrior exhibits himself to the best advantage; here he is at home, and his skill in various manoeuvers which he makes available in battle —such as throwing himself entirely upon one side of his horse and discharging his arrows with great rapidity toward the opposite side from beneath the animal's neck while he is at full speed—is truly astonishing. . . . Every warrior has his war-horse, which is the fleetest that can be obtained, and he prizes him more highly than anything else in his possession, and it is seldom that he can be induced to part with him at any price.

Farming tribes along the borders of the Plains found the horses almost as valuable as did their brothers to the west. They began to range farther from home in a seminomadic state for several months of each year, subsisting more on meat and less on corn. Added mobility increased their trading area and gave them a greater variety of goods. Some of them even gave up their old ways entirely and became true nomads of the Plains.

Chief among these wanderers were the Sioux. They are usually considered the typical Indian tribe of the northern Plains, yet as late as 1766 at least one large band of Sioux still lived in the lake and swamp district of Minnesota. They used bark huts for shelter and canoes for transportation; wild rice furnished most of their food. Within the next decade they gave up their canoes for horses, and their wild rice for buffalo. They moved out to the grasslands of North Dakota and developed spectacular riding costumes topped with the famous Sioux war bonnet.

This late acquisition of horses by the Yankton Sioux emphasizes the relatively slow northward movement of the horse frontier on the Great Plains. Many thousands of animals were needed to fill those vast grazing lands and to supply the numerous large tribes. Winter storms and fierce wolves took heavy toll of the colts, so most of the increase of the herds depended on fresh stock from the New Mexico ranches.

West of the Continental Divide the horse moved northward more rapidly. Here the Indians were few in number, and in the central areas their small valleys furnished scant pasture; hence within thirty years or so, the horses had moved north of Great Salt Lake to the fine stock ranges of the upper Snake Valley, where

they multiplied rapidly. Here they had ample protection from the winter storms and predators were less of a problem than on the Plains. Even the desert plateau furnished ample forage in the winter when storms filled the water holes. This was the country of the western Shoshone, who in time furnished stock to all their neighbors, especially to the Crows, Blackfeet, and Nez Percé.

Once the Nez Percé secured some breeding stock they found that their country was even better for raising range horses than the upper Snake Valley. With excellent grass, ample water, and both summer and winter ranges, it cost them little effort to raise more horses than they could use. They learned to geld some of their poorer stallions, and this practice, combined with their fine range land, produced horses of superior quality.

Up to this time the Nez Percé had been a fishing tribe, living in about fifty small, permanent villages along the Snake River and its tributaries, the Clearwater and the Salmon. Once they learned to use horses, they became more adventurous. They opened a trail along the timbered ridges of the Bitterroot Range to reach the buffalo herds of Montana more than a hundred miles away. In Montana they soon met the Crows and Blackfeet, and later the Sioux. From each they borrowed items of Plains culture, until they had more in common with the Plains Indians than they did with their old neighbors in the fishing villages to the west.

From their ample herds the Nez Percé eventually supplied horses to all their neighbors—at a price, of course. Each year they would ride out to the various intertribal trading grounds with some of their excess stock. One such center was a hundred miles north of the Snake River, on the small plain where the Little Spokane River joins the main stream a few miles below the falls. Since the Spokanes and the Nez Percé were of different language groups, the bartering had to be carried on principally by signs. Each usual article of trade, including the average horse, had an established value, yet the trading was a leisurely process.

The Nez Percé lined up on one side, each man holding the lead rope of his "trading" horse. Each Spokane came forward and placed his pile of trade goods in front of the horse he liked. If the Nez Percé was satisfied, he handed over the lead rope and took the goods. If not, he might try for an extra article, or he might lead his horse to some other pile which interested him. It might take all of a pleasant summer day to trade forty horses, but this seemed to worry nobody.

The Nez Percé also traded horses as far west as The Dalles, and as far east as the Crow country in southern Montana. Later they traded mounts to the fur companies, and to travellers on the Oregon Trail.

George Catlin, the great painter of Indians in the early West, made an entry in his journal in 1834 that epitomizes what the horse did for the Indian. The artist had just encountered his first Comanches, and he soon concluded that they were the most extraordinary horsemen in the world. Dismounted, he wrote, they were "heavy and ungraceful . . . one of the most unattractive and slovenly-looking races of Indians that I have ever seen; but the moment they mount their horses, they seem at once metamorphosed, and surprise the spectator with the ease and elegance of their movements. A Camanchee on his feet is out of his element, and comparatively almost as awkward as a monkey on the ground, without a limb or a branch to cling to; but the moment he lays his hand upon his horse, his *face,* even, becomes handsome, and he gracefully flies away like a different being."

One of the Spanish conquistadors, in the sixteenth century, had observed confidently: "Horses are what the Indians dread most, and by means of which they will be overcome." He failed to foresee that the Indians would make the horse their own, and that thereby their native culture would not only be tremendously enhanced, but would flourish for over a hundred years before their warriors would be crushed by the advancing Anglo-Americans.

Dr. Haines, a well-known authority on the Nez Percé Indians, teaches social science at Oregon College of Education. His most recent book is Appaloosa: The Spotted Horse in Art and History *(University of Texas, 1963).*
For further reading: The Indian and the Horse, *by Frank Roe (University of Oklahoma Press, 1955).*

"The most unpopular man in the north" CONTINUED FROM PAGE 14

bling Congress, and for capriciously overlooking the fact that the Constitution empowers Congress, and Congress alone, to raise and support armies. Yet the President, without prior legislative sanction, had created his own army—a course which if pursued by an English sovereign within the last two centuries, Vallandigham noted, would have resulted in the loss of his head. In his unsparing attacks upon the administration, however, he seemed to make no allowance whatever for the gravity of the nation's peril and the need for drastic and immediate action.

Vallandigham's concerns were by no means limited to the floor of the House of Representatives, for he was heavily engaged in politics at home. In Ohio, as in many another state of the West and East, there were in reality two Democratic parties. The War Democrats advocated vigorous prosecution of the war to restore the Federal Union at the earliest possible moment. Opposed to them were the Peace Democrats—or the Copperheads, as they were called by their detractors—who included Vallandigham, his fellow Ohio congressmen George H. Pendleton and Samuel S. Cox, former Governor Thomas Hart Seymour of Connecticut, and Fernando Wood, the charming but ruthless mayor of New York City. Even in Copperhead circles, Vallandigham was considered an extremist.

Vallandigham was essentially a sectional politician whose doctrines were a compound of local interest and local circumstance. In Ohio, he was the hero of the poor farmer, who, typically, had emigrated from the South, tilled substandard soil, owned a shabby home-

stead, and was apt to be illiterate. In Dayton, Cincinnati, Columbus, and other Ohio cities, Vallandigham was a favorite of the recent Irish and German immigrants, and particularly of the unskilled laborers among them. Farmers and workingmen feared that the freeing of the Negro would unloose a great flood of cheap labor that would engulf the West and drive them out of their meager employments. To these people who dreaded the changes that the war might bring, his constant electioneering slogan, "The Constitution as it is, the Union as it was," had special point. To Vallandigham, righteous New England abolitionists and greedy, high-tariff eastern capitalists were responsible for the nation's misery. Next to the West, his sympathies lay with the South. He was impressed with the prowess of her arms, and as the war proceeded, he expressed repeatedly in his speeches unconcealed satisfaction in her victories and grave doubts concerning the ability of Union armies ultimately to prevail.

The year 1862 subjected Vallandigham to the crucial test of re-election. The prospects for victory, as he and his most ardent followers recognized, were exceedingly poor. His congressional district had been recently gerrymandered by the newly constituted Union party (or what Vallandigham called the "no party"), an amalgam of the Republicans and the War Democrats, which now controlled the Ohio legislature. The gerrymander had added to his district a new county, Warren, one of the state's abolitionist strongholds.

Despite the bleak prospects, Vallandigham campaigned hard. He crisscrossed his district, speaking at country picnics and on city street corners. His vehement oratory and showmanship enormously intrigued the crowds.

For all this effort, the returns on election day showed conclusively that the gerrymander had served its purpose. Vallandigham went down to defeat. Although he carried the original counties of his district by a larger vote than ever before, he lost heavily in the gerrymandered county, Warren. But Vallandigham's setback resulted in no noticeable diminution of his political stock. The gerrymander had added a new dimension to his martyrdom, and in one Copperhead county after another, resolutions were adopted urging his nomination for governor in the 1863 election.

Preliminary soundings made by Vallandigham upon his return to Ohio from Washington in 1863 revealed that a majority of the state's Democratic leaders were opposed to his nomination for the governorship. Clearly he needed a dramatic and meaningful issue to build up a massive public support that the party professionals could not ignore. An ideal opportunity suddenly materialized in the person and policies of the newly appointed resident Union commander, General Ambrose E. Burnside. Tactless, impetuous, and smarting under his recent disastrous defeat at the Battle of Fredericksburg, Burnside had been sent to Ohio to halt a series of disorders attributed to the Copperheads. The General proceeded to issue a series of freedom-curbing orders which, among other things, forbade the citizenry to keep and bear arms and to speak out publicly against administration policies. The best known of Burnside's several edicts was "General Order No. 38" of April 13, 1863, with its broad and loosely defined decree that those who committed "acts for the benefit of our enemies" would be tried by military tribunal "as spies or traitors."

In one address after another, Vallandigham excoriated the Burnside orders as the ultimate in Lincolnian despotism. The most consequential of Vallandigham's angry expositions was delivered at Mount Vernon, Ohio, on May 4 before a crowd estimated at 20,000. It was for Vallandigham a mild speech until he came inevitably to speak of Burnside's Order No. 38 and dissolved into a fit of rhetorical rage. He "despised it," he shouted, "spit upon it, trampled it under his feet." The crowd roared back its defiant approval. While Vallandigham spoke, a captain of the Union volunteers in plain clothes was leaning against the speakers' platform, taking down his words in shorthand.

Late that same night, General Burnside dispatched a force to arrest Vallandigham. Awakened at 2:30 A.M. by a violent knocking on the door, the Copperhead went to a front upstairs window, not suspecting what was afoot. In an instant he knew. The tramp of armed

On May 25, 1863, Union soldiers under a flag of truce deposited

men, the low voice of command, the rattling of arms, the bayonets glittering in the gaslight, could mean but one thing: his arrest.

As Vallandigham threw open the shutters, his wife screamed with fright. The captain in command announced his purpose. Vallandigham shouted that no military officer had the lawful right to arrest him. Unless Vallandigham came down, replied the captain, he would be shot. The beleaguered Copperhead shouted for the police. There was a moment of silence, an angry command, and the house began to shake as the blows of axes broke down its doors. One soon gave way, and a wave of cursing men carrying bayonets surged inside. Vallandigham retreated through several rooms before he was finally encircled by a score of pointed rifles. He was quickly marched to a railroad depot and taken by special train to Cincinnati.

Vallandigham's arrest put Dayton into an uproar. By noon the next day, wagons and carriages crammed with his followers were pouring into the city. At twilight a mob of five hundred men, hooting and yelling, sacked the office of the Dayton *Journal,* a Unionist publication. Stones and bullets shattered the newspaper's windows and blazing torches were hurled inside. The fire raced through three stores, a meat market, a livery stable, and the office of a church publication. The city's firemen, their engines sabotaged and their hoses slashed, fought helplessly.

The charges against Vallandigham were based

Vallandigham (center) within Rebel lines near Murfreesboro, Tenn.

mainly on his speech at Mount Vernon. There he was alleged to have called the war "wicked, cruel, and unnecessary," claiming that it was fought "for the purpose of crushing out Liberty and erecting a Despotism," that it was "a war for the freedom of the blacks and the enslavement of the whites," and that "if the Administration had wished, the war could have been honorably terminated months ago." By these and other statements, the charges continued, Vallandigham had violated General Order No. 38.

The day following his arrest, Vallandigham was brought to trial before a military commission of eight officers. When the court convened, Vallandigham calmly stated that the commission lacked authority to try him. He was not a member of the armed forces, he pointed out, and was therefore subject only to the civil judiciary. The trial nevertheless proceeded, the shorthand notes were introduced, and Vallandigham was found guilty of the charges against him. Appeals on his part to the United States Court for the Southern District of Ohio and eventually to the Supreme Court were to no avail.

Inside the Lincoln administration, opinion was less unanimous than it was among the military judges. "The proceedings," wrote Secretary of the Navy Gideon Welles, echoing the feelings of the President, "were arbitrary and injudicious. It gives bad men the right of questions, an advantage of which they avail themselves.

Good men, who wish to support the Administration, find it difficult to defend these acts." The arrest, trial, and sentencing of Vallandigham, in point of fact, had taken Lincoln rather by surprise. Once faced with an accomplished fact, however, he had to decide whether to approve the military court's decision or to annul it, thereby weakening the commanding general's authority in his district and encouraging the anti-administration element throughout the West. Lincoln chose to back up Burnside; and then, with a finesse truly indicative of his political genius, proceeded to go one step further. He wisely concluded that Vallandigham's incarceration would only refuel the fires of popular sympathy for the Copperhead, establishing a lasting source of irritation and public discussion. Instead, Lincoln chose to hand Vallandigham over to the Confederates, thus pinning upon him a contemptible and indelible badge of affiliation with the enemies of his country. So Vallandigham was hustled on board the United States gunboat *Exchange* at Cincinnati and taken down the Ohio River to Louisville; from there, he was escorted under heavy guard to Murfreesboro, the advanced headquarters of the Union Army in Tennessee. On the morning of May 25, following his brief debate with General Rosecrans on loyalty, the Copperhead was deposited behind Confederate lines.

Vallandigham's stay in the South was not passed in idleness—though a good deal of controversy still surrounds his exact activities. Some evidence suggests that his days were devoted to one of the most heinous pursuits known to man, treason. Vallandigham was extensively interviewed by leading Confederate officials and, according to some accounts, he played a vital part in persuading the Confederates to undertake two major military enterprises in the summer of 1863. One was nothing less than General Robert E. Lee's invasion of Pennsylvania, and the other was General John Hunt Morgan's daring raid into the Ohio Valley. These ventures were encouraged, said Confederate Captain Joe Lane, by Vallandigham's insistence that the North was "ripe for revolution" and only waited upon the appearance of Southern armies to overturn Lincoln and proclaim for Jefferson Davis.

A wholly opposite view of Vallandigham's conduct is provided by Colonel Robert Ould, who interviewed the exile on behalf of the Confederate President. According to Ould's account of their conversation, Vallandigham had begged the South to drop plans it was then readying to invade Pennsylvania. An invasion, Vallandigham warned, would unite the parties of the North, dissolve all popular support for the Peace Democrats, and immeasurably strengthen Lincoln's hand in suppressing political dissent.

However much Vallandigham's activities may be in

dispute, it is clear that he chose to leave the Confederacy at the earliest possible moment to take up exile in Canada, "where I can see my family, communicate with my friends & transact my business as far as practicable, unmolested." The Confederates assented to this plan.

On June 17, 1863, Vallandigham set out for his new land by a circuitous route. He sailed from Wilmington, North Carolina, on the British steamer *Cornubia,* bound for Bermuda, where he arrived on June 20; a coterie of Confederate agents were his fellow passengers. Midway in the trip, a dire crisis materialized in the shape of an approaching Union man-of-war. The *Cornubia*'s terror-stricken captain turned to his most famous (or infamous) passenger, Vallandigham, for counsel. Were there British soldiers' uniforms on board? that seasoned veteran of crisis calmly inquired. Fortunately there were some, presumably destined for the British garrison on Bermuda. At Vallandigham's suggestion, the crew and the Confederate agents quickly donned the uniforms. The hasty recruits paraded with nervous inexactitude around the deck; and apparently convinced that the *Cornubia* was a British troopship, the man-of-war changed course.

After ten days in Bermuda, Vallandigham and several dozen Confederate agents embarked on another British steamer, the *Harriet Pinckney,* for Halifax, Nova Scotia. This leg of the journey also entailed several harrowing brushes with Union frigates and anxious groping through dense Atlantic fog banks; finally they reached Halifax on July 5. Vallandigham immediately pushed on to Quebec and Montreal, where he received official welcomes. He resided briefly at Clifton House on the Canadian side of Niagara Falls and then settled at Windsor, Ontario. Situated opposite Detroit, Windsor was in easy reach of Ohio and the rest of the Midwest. Vallandigham occupied a comfortable second-story apartment facing the Detroit River. He had a fine view of the town and of the United States gunboat *Michigan,* which had moved into position upon his arrival, with its guns trained directly upon his living room.

Vallandigham's chief business in his new location was to promote his candidacy for the governorship of Ohio. He had already been nominated by the Democratic state convention—his martyrdom had clinched it—and the campaign was in full swing. His opponent, John Brough, a founder of the Cincinnati *Enquirer,* a stellar outdoor orator, and a War Democrat, had been nominated by that wing of the party and also by the Republicans.

Despite a hard-fought campaign, the election's outcome was starkly foreshadowed by magnificent victories of the Union at Gettysburg and Vicksburg; they obliterated much of the lack of confidence in the Lincoln administration, on which Vallandigham's popularity long had thrived. When the returns on election day were finally totalled, the Copperhead had lost by an unprecedented majority.

While Vallandigham was nursing the wounds of defeat, the stock of another Ohioan, General George B. McClellan, was booming as the prospective Democratic nominee for the Presidency in 1864. Relieved of the command of the Army of the Potomac on November 7, 1862, the dawdling general was available. Alarmed by the possibility of a presidential candidate with a military background, a group of midwestern Peace Democrats decided to consult with Vallandigham at Windsor. The visitors had a second and not unrelated matter to take up with him: the organization of a newborn secret society, the Sons of Liberty, which conceivably might be manipulated to block McClellan and build up another candidate—hopefully a staunch Peace Democrat.

The several predecessors of the Sons of Liberty had been pure anathema to the Lincoln administration. All were Copperhead organizations, pro-Southern in orientation, and capable of great mischief. These earlier societies were deemed responsible for the huge shipments of arms into anti-Union hands in Indiana in 1863 and for the tumultuous resistance to the draft in that state and in Illinois.

When the delegation of Peace Democrats reached Windsor, it proffered Vallandigham the supreme commandership of the Sons of Liberty. According to his own account of the interview, he at first declined, saying he was opposed in principle to secret societies. His callers pointed out, however, that the Republicans already had formed their own secret societies, the highly effective Union Leagues, to bring out the party vote, watch over the polls, and forestall possible violence. Vallandigham finally accepted, but with one condition: the Society's activities must be "kept legitimate and lawful." His visitors quickly assured him that the group "was only a political organization having reference to affairs in the States that had adhered to the Union and recognized the Federal Government and its authorities." When Vallandigham was invited to suggest an oath for his fellow members, he proposed (he later asserted) that it include a pledge to support the Constitution of the United States.

Unfortunately, what is known of Vallandigham's further Canadian activities seems to run directly counter to his protestations of loyalty to the Union. Following his investiture as supreme commander of the Sons of Liberty, he was visited by several representatives of the Confederacy. They did not just happen by; they came to Canada expressly to see him. With the war now going badly for their cause, high-ranking Confederate officials had begun to think, with a boldness born of desperation, of fomenting uprisings in the most disaffected areas of the Midwest. The uprisings were part of a larger plan aimed at securing the release of 30,000 to 50,000 Confederate soldiers in Union prison camps in Indiana and Illinois. In April of 1864, Jefferson Davis, who enthusiastically endorsed the project, appointed three commissioners, headed by Jacob Thompson, to proceed to Canada with some $900,000. The money was to be used to bring about the release of the prisoners, to destroy Union military and naval stores, to influence the press, and to purchase arms for the several secret political societies, including the Sons of Liberty.

On June 9, 1864, Thompson's deputy, the twenty-three-year-old Captain Thomas H. Hines, who had recently won Southern acclaim by escaping with General John Hunt Morgan from an Ohio prison, visited Vallandigham at Windsor. Two days later, Jacob Thompson himself met with Vallandigham. According to Confederate accounts of the conversations, Vallandigham talked principally of the power and size of the Sons of Liberty in Indiana, Illinois, and Ohio. Somewhere in his discourse, Vallandigham contended that if the Confederates supplied the society with a sufficient quantity of money and arms, it could successfully overthrow the existing governments of Illinois, Indiana, Ohio, and Kentucky. In such an event, these several states would be converted at once into a western confederacy, separate and independent from both the North and the South. It was a conspiratorial dream which far exceeded Jeff Davis' original aspirations, and the Confederate agents eagerly proffered their money. But, still asserting his unwillingness to identify with the Southern cause, Vallandigham declined to accept it personally. He recommended that it be entrusted instead to Dr. James A. Barrett of St. Louis, grand lecturer of the Sons of Liberty.

Late in June of 1864, with the presidential election approaching, Vallandigham decided that he must chance a return to the United States at all costs. For this necessarily furtive undertaking, he put on a disguise. His eyebrows became heavier and darker; a thick mustache swept his upper lip; a flowing beard fell to his waist; and a large concealed pillow provided Falstaffian girth. He boarded a regular Canadian passenger boat and landed safely at Detroit, only to encounter an anxious moment when a conscientious customs official poked him in his pillowed abdomen. "Pardon me," said the official, "I see I am mistaken, but I have to watch for tricks." Vallandigham moved on. He reached Hamilton, Ohio, just in time to be chosen by the Democratic convention of the third congressional district, which was gathered there, as a delegate to the future presidential convention.

Vallandigham quickly announced his presence by launching into a series of public speeches in Dayton, Syracuse, and New York City that, if anything, were more violent than those which had brought about his arrest. He still hammered at his old theme, the summoning of a convention of all the states to arrange a peace settlement restoring "the union as it was." Intermixed with his proposal were ringing defiances of the Lincoln government and veiled but unmistakable threats that in the event of his rearrest those respon-

"War and Argument—Cold Steel and Cool Reason—having failed to restore the Union," said Harper's, *in a swipe at the Peace Democrats, "it is supposed that the South may be* bored *into coming back."*

sible would be taken hostage by his supporters. But for all of Vallandigham's cacophony, the administration left him alone. It would be better, the President felt, to let the man's intemperate words discredit the Democratic party.

When the Democratic national convention assembled in Chicago on August 29, Vallandigham's immediate endeavors were focussed upon the resolutions committee, of which he was a member. After meeting into the early morning hours, the committee brought to the floor a brief platform of six planks, the second of which Vallandigham had prepared and forced through by a narrow vote. He rightly characterized his plank as the most "material" of the Chicago platform. It was a "peace plank," encouraged by Grant's current involvement in the long, costly, and indecisive struggle with Lee in Virginia, which was reawakening the old doubts concerning the wisdom of the struggle. After scoring the failure of the war and the Lincoln administration's violations of constitutional liberty and private rights, the plank urged an immediate cessation of hostilities and the calling of a convention of the states "to the end that at the earliest practicable moment peace may be restored on the basis of the Federal Union of the States." Vallandigham's plank was promptly adopted.

The next order of business was the nomination of General George B. McClellan, the party's best vote-getter, for President, an act of supreme paradox. Having declared for peace and nominated a general, the delegates had created a glaring contradiction. Which of these two acts constituted the more authoritative expression of the true position of the Democratic party? Although Vallandigham pressed McClellan hard to stand by the peace plank, the General all but repudiated it by calling for union, and therefore victory, as a prerequisite of peace. His subsequent campaign fired little enthusiasm in Vallandigham and, for that matter, in the Union as a whole. Lincoln swept to an easy victory. In Ohio political circles the question evoking more attention than the election was whether the Lincoln administration, safely entrenched in power for another four years, would again arrest Vallandigham.

Even before the Democrats nominated a presidential candidate at Chicago, more sinister events had been taking place behind the scenes. As Grant and Sherman drove deeper into Southern territory in the summer of 1864, Confederate demands upon the Sons of Liberty to commence the uprisings plotted in the several Canadian meetings became increasingly intense. Further meetings of Confederate representatives and Sons of Liberty leaders were held: one at St. Catherines, Ontario, on July 22, another at London, Ontario, on August 7. Although Vallandigham did not participate in either, federal agents who were watching the situation closely asserted that the selection of a specific date in August for launching the uprisings was left to him. Vallandigham, for his part, always denied having any knowledge of the conspiracy; he was, he said, in New York State at the time when his decision was supposedly required. Confederate records disclose that ultimately several dates had been selected, but in each instance, as the hour for action approached, the Sons of Liberty concluded that more time was needed.

Despite the several postponements, the Confederate agents looked forward hopefully to the Chicago presidential convention. Hungry for success, they demanded that a well-stocked "transportation fund," previously entrusted to Dr. Barrett, be expended to bring some 50,000 members of the Sons of Liberty to Chicago. Several days before the convention began, sixty Confederate soldiers, armed and in plain clothes, and led by Captains Thomas Hines and John B. Castleman, slipped into the city by way of Canada. The Confederates put up at the same hotel where Vallandigham and his associates were staying.

Arms would be provided to the Sons of Liberty men; under the supervision of the Confederates, they would assault nearby Camp Douglas and Rock Island, Illinois, to release many thousands of Confederate prisoners held at those places. As the zero hour approached, the Copperhead leaders got their customary attack of cold feet; the venture was dropped. The forte of Vallandigham and his colleagues, in the Confederates' estimation, was "governmental theory." It was not revolution.

The Lincoln administration, whose agents had deftly infiltrated the higher echelons of the Sons of Liberty, was fully informed of events in Chicago. On the basis of these reports, the administration conceivably might have rearrested Vallandigham. But it did not. Nevertheless, certain arrests of lesser-known participants were made, and when the accused were brought to trial before a military commission nearly a year after the Chicago convention, Vallandigham was a voluntary defense witness, but disclaimed personal knowledge of the plot.

Felix G. Stidger, a resourceful federal agent who infiltrated the Sons of Liberty with such success that he became grand secretary of the order in the state of Kentucky, minimized Vallandigham's part in the Chicago conspiracy. Although Stidger did not corroborate Vallandigham's claim of ignorance, he carefully excluded the Copperhead from his list of the malefactors. "Vallandigham," Stidger wrote of the plot to seize arsenals and release prisoners, "took *no active part* in any of this work; and even his suggestions and advice were *overruled* by the *Active Working Head* of the Order, Harrison H. Dodd, of Indianapolis."

DEDICATED TO THE CHICAGO CONVENTION.

In the Chicago Democratic convention's call for a compromise peace with the South, Thomas Nast saw only the ruin of a war fought to no purpose. He pictured a future in which the Union was degraded, the bondage of the Negro made permanent, and the brutal ascendancy of the slaveholder assured.

Was Vallandigham a misguided zealot or an opportunistic politician who turned to treason to further his own career? The evidence of several crucial episodes—in the Confederacy, in Canada, at Chicago—on which the question turns, is admittedly conflicting. But imperfect evidence cannot rescue Vallandigham from the most damaging weakness of his position: the repeated necessity for explaining his involvement in occurrences that smell of treason. The fact that one situation after another, whether in Ohio, in the South, in Canada, or in other places, has to be excused or justified withers confidence in him. Good men do not consort repeatedly with the enemy and his agents of subversion. They do not accept his money, even indirectly. Nor do they retain the leadership of organizations whose controlling elements practice treason.

If phases of Vallandigham's undercover enterprises are obscure, his visible activities, represented by his speeches, are not. Steadily, month in and month out, the guarded but all-too-transparent incitement to revolt, to secede, or otherwise to resist federal authority falls from his lips into the willing ears of his followers. No government can well tolerate such conduct if it is to survive, least of all if it is locked in civil war.

When the Civil War ended, Vallandigham labored to restore his party's badly lagging national fortunes by revising its policy positions in light of the new realities. The original scene of his not-inconsiderable enterprise was the Democratic convention of Montgomery County which assembled at Dayton on May 18, 1871; there a series of resolutions, drafted under Vallandigham's leadership, and known as "The New Departure," were adopted. Among other things, they called for a general amnesty for the vanquished South, curtailment of the Ku Klux Klan, a merit system for the civil service, and a tax structure based upon wealth rather than population. Vallandigham's resolutions were received with general approbation in the West and East. The New York *Sun,* in an opinion typical of the eastern press,

now placed Vallandigham "among the most conspicuous political leaders of the day." The New Departure was indeed giving the Democratic party a new start by releasing it, at long last, from the old war issues to which it had so tenaciously and so unprofitably clung. Vallandigham was the first Democrat of the postwar years to come forward with a program that faced the formidable new problems of the day, attracted national support, and restored his party to serious contention in presidential and congressional elections.

It was during his promotion of the New Departure that Vallandigham was engaged as defense attorney for a Thomas McGehan, accused of murder in a fatal saloon brawl in Hamilton, Ohio. In the course of demonstrating with a loaded revolver his theory that the slain man had shot himself, Vallandigham accidentally pulled the trigger. There was a sudden crack and flash. Reeling toward a wall and exclaiming, "My God, I've shot myself," Vallandigham fell, mortally wounded. (Happily, his unstinting dedication to the case contributed to McGehan's subsequent acquittal.)

Vallandigham lingered briefly, and died on June 17, 1871, at the age of fifty-one. Sometime after his passing, his fellow warrior of Copperhead days, George Pendleton, expressed a thought that must have struck Vallandigham in his anguish. "I thank God," said Pendleton, "he has lived long enough to see that Time, the Avenger in whom he had such unwavering faith, has commenced his work, and that many who had maligned him most were beginning to see their error and to do him justice."

A three-time contributor to AMERICAN HERITAGE, *Louis W. Koenig is professor of government at New York University. He is the author of a well-known study of presidential confidants,* The Invisible Presidency.

For further reading: The Copperheads in the Middle West, *by Frank L. Klement (University of Chicago, 1960), and* Abraham Lincoln and the Fifth Column, *by George F. Milton (Collier, 1962).*

A Foot in the Door CONTINUED FROM PAGE 48

to secure their corner the speculators would have to buy up all the grain. They turned to Chicago's banks for a million-dollar loan, but were unsuccessful: their credit was already severely stretched. They had to stop buying, and wheat prices plummeted forty-seven cents in a twenty-four-hour period. Munn & Scott was ruined, its grain receipts thoroughly discredited. To avoid a complete panic, the powerful George Armour & Co. bought the Munn interests and quietly set about purchasing grain to make its receipts good. Munn and

Scott themselves went into bankruptcy; the ensuing court proceedings, as summarized in newspaper headlines, told the story of the Chicago elevator business: IRA Y. MUNN ON STAND LAYS BARE ELEVATOR COMBINATION—PROFITS DIVIDED—AGREEMENT IN 1866—A GENERAL POOL—HISTORY OF CONTRACTS WITH NORTHWESTERN RAILWAY BEGINNING IN 1862 AND RENEWED IN 1866.

The sequel came on December 3, 1872, when Munn and Scott were expelled from the Board of Trade.

Although Ira Munn and George Scott passed into oblivion, the regulatory impulse that they and their fellow warehousemen had helped trigger continued unabated. The year 1873 was one of economic panic; grain prices dropped further, and a severe shortage of credit forced numerous mortgage foreclosures. The Granger movement reached floodtide, and its political power was felt in all the midwestern states. Granger votes elected legislators and governors who helped pass laws lowering railroad rates; as the Minnesota governor inelegantly put it, "It is time to take robber corporations by the scruff of the neck and shake them over hell!"

The Granger laws, cursed as communistic in eastern business and financial circles, were a tribute to the political power of organized farmers. But, having failed to prevent the new legislation, the railroads retaliated with a variety of weapons. Their agents fought to repeal or weaken the laws and to persuade the public of their undesirability. They insisted that regulation would discourage further rail construction—an effective point, for even the bitterest foes of "the octopus" wanted increased railroad service at a fair price.

Resistance took other forms as well. In some cases the roads aimed to make the laws backfire: because of technical loopholes they were able to equalize their rates (thus formally ending discriminations) by *raising* them as much as fifty per cent in areas where they had been low. In other cases, they reduced service and forecast its complete abandonment. Wisconsin customers, for example, were subjected to dilapidated cars and erratic service that the railroads suavely blamed on the unusually harsh regulations of the Potter law—"Potter cars, Potter rails, and Potter time."

Mostly, however, the corporations put their faith in the judiciary—not the elective state courts where decisions were likely to mirror popular desires, but the United States Supreme Court. The railroads were supremely confident that rate regulation, no matter how moderate, violated the Constitution for at least three reasons. The first was that the laws contravened the federal contract clause by impairing their right to set rates, a right granted by the states' charters of incorporation. Here the railroads cited the Dartmouth College doctrine of 1819 (see Richard N. Current's article in the August, 1963, AMERICAN HERITAGE). (They conveniently overlooked the Supreme Court's later ruling in the Charles River Bridge Case, which modified the doctrine on the ground that the public also had rights and that these could be bargained away only by an *explicit* grant. Furthermore, the railroads' charters had been issued under state constitutions which contained clauses reserving the legislatures'

authority to amend them.) Second, the corporations urged that rate regulation tampered with interstate transportation, thereby impinging on Congress' plenary power over interstate commerce. Lastly, they argued that public rate-setting was a radical innovation unknown in the American experience. It was, they contended, a confiscation which violated the Fourteenth Amendment's prohibition against depriving persons of their property without due process of law.

Corporation resistance quickly led to specific cases in the state and lower federal courts. The Chicago warehousemen who had by now succeeded to the Munn & Scott properties continued to defy the Warehouse Act and carried their case to the state supreme court—unsuccessfully. The state, declared the Illinois judges, might regulate all subjects "connected with the public welfare" in order "to promote the greatest good of the greatest number."

Despite this and other reverses in the lower courts, the business interests were confident of ultimate victory. The assurances of their high-priced legal talent were soothing, and the corporations appealed their cases. In 1873 and 1874 *Munn v. Illinois* and seven railroad cases, which became known as the Granger Railroad Cases, all made their way to the United States Supreme Court, and, so the railroad leaders felt, toward a decision favorable to business.

Their confidence, however, was grossly misplaced. The Court of the 1870's did not regard itself as the judicial handmaiden to entrepreneurial capitalism. Its Chief Justice, Morrison Remick Waite, was a moderate whose deep faith in representative democracy made him tolerant of legislative experimentation. His attitude had been shaped in frontier Ohio, where he had settled in 1838. His politics were solidly Republican, and his experiences in a close-knit community where personal honesty and character mattered as much as business acumen made Waite a typical member of the ante-bellum class of professional and mercantile men to whom wealth was not an end in itself.

Ironically, this man of complete integrity was appointed to the Chief Justiceship through the tawdry maneuverings of the Grant era. When a vacancy occurred in the office in 1873, President Grant tried to please his malodorous entourage with three dubious candidates, but was forced by public outcry to withdraw each in turn. The muddled President then looked for an honest man and found Waite, whose obscure respectability assured his confirmation. An unassuming middle-aged lawyer of medium height, his face clothed in one of those ample beards that were the style of his day, Waite proved himself a first-rate judge

89

The rapidly swelling power of the Grangers was signalled by the crowds that turned out to regional meetings to voice their grievances and demand reform legislation. Above, several thousand gather at Edwardsville, Illinois, in September, 1873.

and an excellent Chief Justice. While his intelligence was keen, his most valuable assets were an amiable personality and a knack for leading men. "Policy" and "diplomacy" were his self-proclaimed guidelines.

These qualities served him well. Waite's associates were men of uncommon ability, but their vanities and ambitions could easily have mired the Court in a morass of personal conflicts. Unquestionably the best mind and the most learned jurist among them was Joseph P. Bradley. A self-made man, Bradley enjoyed a successful career representing some of New Jersey's leading railroads until appointed to the Court in 1870 by President Grant. Once on the bench, he showed marked independence toward the corporate interests he had formerly defended, frequently upholding economic regulation. Another Court giant was Samuel Freeman Miller. Beginning as a poor Kentucky farm boy, Miller had had two careers, one as a rural doctor and, after studying law on his own, another as a country lawyer. Appointed by Lincoln in 1862, Miller habitually stressed the importance of personal liberties and reflected a hostility to corporate and financial wealth. Blunt, self-confident, and prone to vanity, he was a

dominant figure on the Court after the Civil War.

Ward Hunt, Noah H. Swayne, Nathan Clifford, and David Davis, four of the tribunal's lesser lights, generally followed Waite's lead in economic regulation cases. Like Waite, all of them had grown to maturity in Jacksonian America, and they retained a democratic faith that made them favorably disposed to laws passed by the people's representatives.

The remaining two associate justices were exceptions. William Strong was a conservative, sympathetic to corporation views. Stephen J. Field, whose brother Cyrus laid the Atlantic cable, was a transplanted New Englander who prided himself on being a rugged Californian. Through a judicial service of nearly thirty-five years Field outspokenly defended the claims of American business.

Judicial processes are rarely speedy, and the Court of the seventies moved with majestic slowness. Overburdened with a lengthy docket, it required an average of three years to announce decisions. The first Granger case to reach the Court, a challenge to Minnesota's rate law, arrived in October, 1873, and the Illinois, Iowa, and Wisconsin cases were docketed the next year. Oral

90

arguments occupied two sessions during the 1875 term; the Granger Railroad Cases were heard in October, 1875, and *Munn v. Illinois,* the elevator case, was argued early in 1876.

For the oral arguments the business interests marshalled the elite of the nation's bar. William M. Evarts, Orville H. Browning, David Dudley Field (another brother of Justice Field's), and Frederick T. Frelinghuysen were among the assembled legal talent. They strongly argued the three contentions advanced by their side in the lower courts: confiscation of property, impairment of contract obligations, and interference with interstate commerce. To these constitutional arguments they added that rate regulation was almost unheard of in America, and that the Granger laws were "the beginning of the operations of the [Paris] commune in the legislation of this country." In reply, the attorneys for the state governments involved defended the laws as reasonable measures to protect the general welfare against the exactions of private, uncurbed monopolies whose business had in effect become public.

Despite the brilliance of the railroad attorneys and the eloquence of their arguments, seven of the Supreme Court justices cast their votes for the Granger laws. Only Field and Strong dissented on November 18, 1876, when all eight cases were decided together. Chief Justice Waite assigned himself the opinions, well aware of their importance; this was the Court's first major statement on the constitutionality of regulating the new industrial capitalism. He chose the elevator case, *Munn v. Illinois,* for his main opinion. Unlike the companies involved in the Granger Railroad Cases, Munn and Scott were unincorporated partners and their business was not directly involved in interstate transportation. Their case therefore presented the crucial issue, the permissibility of rate regulation, in pure form, uncomplicated by the contract and commerce questions raised in the other disputes.

The Chief Justice devoted the winter to preparing the opinions, later remarking that "they kept my mind and hands at work all the time." Waite did his opinion-writing at home, sitting at a long and cluttered library table in his private study, where he worked in the morning's early hours and often into the night. Admittedly old-fashioned, he spurned secretaries and the newfangled typewriter, making his drafts in longhand. A glimpse of his labors on the *Munn* opinion is preserved on a lined sheet of paper on which he jotted down earlier illustrations of American business regulation. These references to historical practice, some of which appeared in the final opinion, were pertinent. The parties challenging the Granger laws had strongly contended that regulation was alien to America; to demolish their claim Waite naturally referred to the state he knew best, citing precedents from Ohio history.

As Waite prepared the *Munn* opinion, he turned for assistance to Justice Bradley, his closest collaborator on the Court. Bradley in fact deserves recognition as the opinion's co-author: he prepared a lengthy "Outline of my views on the subject of the Granger Cases," from which the Chief Justice freely borrowed. In refuting the business arguments, Bradley, a confirmed legal antiquarian, dug up an obscure seventeenth-century English legal treatise, *De Portibus Maris.* Written by Lord Chief Justice Hale, it justified regulation of the fees charged in public ports with the following language: "For now the wharf and crane and other conveniences are affected with a publick interest, and they cease to be *juris privati* only." Waite quoted this statement and so introduced the public-interest doctrine to a long life in American constitutional law. Late in February he circulated the draft opinions among the brethren for their final approval. Bradley, the former railroad attorney, responded enthusiastically—"terse, correct, & safe." Miller found the opinions "equal to the occasion which is a very great one."

With these endorsements, the Court released its opinions on March 1, 1877, ruling that the Constitution sanctioned economic regulation in the public interest. Waite's opinion in *Munn v. Illinois* began by stressing the power of the Chicago grain elevators, which, standing at the gateway of commerce to the East, "take toll from all who pass." Their business, he argued, citing Lord Hale, "tends to a common charge, and is become a thing of public interest and use" subject to state control. Noting earlier instances of American price regulation, Waite summarily dismissed the contention that such laws unconstitutionally confiscated private property. Underlying these conclusions was the root assumption of *Munn v. Illinois*—that the popularly accountable legislatures should be the judges of the wisdom of regulatory laws. "For protection against abuses by legislatures the people must resort to the polls, not to the courts," Waite wrote, a remark that symbolizes the opinion's status as one of the Supreme Court's major declarations in favor of judicial self-restraint in economic-regulation cases.

With the Warehouse Act sustained, the Granger Railroad Cases fell easily into place. In brief opinions Waite disposed of them by relying on the public-interest doctrine. He rejected the commerce-clause argument, finding that none of the regulations extended to commerce beyond state lines. He found the claim that the rate laws impaired contract rights to be equally without merit; the states' constitutions had reserved the power to amend charters.

Justice Field, as expected, wrote a fiery dissent labelling the *Munn* decision "subversive of the rights of private property" and predicted that its reasoning implied an almost unlimited scope for the regulatory power: "If the power can be exercised as to one article, it may as to all articles, and the prices of everything, from a calico gown to a city mansion, may be the subject of legislative direction." Field's gloomy prediction was essentially correct in calling attention to the broad implications of the *Munn* decision. In modern-day America the scope of governmental regulation is immense; no one doubts that "the prices of everything"— even calico gowns and city mansions—may be regulated. And this intervention by government in economic affairs finds much of its constitutional sanction in *Munn v. Illinois* and in the line of cases which are its progeny.

During the seventies and eighties, the years when Waite and his majority sat on the Court, the public-interest doctrine, and the underlying assumption that legislative acts are valid unless completely arbitrary, led to further expansions of regulatory power. State railroad regulations were repeatedly upheld, as were laws limiting the rates charged by water companies, prohibiting lotteries, and scaling down the interest and principal owed to the holders of state bonds. Congress' power to regulate federally chartered corporations was similarly upheld by a decision, in the Sinking Fund Cases of 1879, which infuriated corporation and financial leaders.

In later judicial periods, roughly between 1895 and 1937, judges far more committed to free enterprise than Waite, Bradley, and Miller often found reasons for invalidating economic regulations in the due-process clauses of the Fifth and Fourteenth amendments. *Munn v. Illinois* was never overruled, but its public-interest doctrine was radically reinterpreted in the 1920's. The conservative Taft Court struck down a number of state regulatory laws as unconstitutional, declaring that only a narrow category of businesses—enterprises traditionally regulated and large monopolies—were affected with a public interest.

All this came to an end in the next decade. In the 1934 case of *Nebbia v. New York,* sustaining a comprehensive scheme of state milk-price regulation, the Supreme Court returned to a sweeping view of the public-interest doctrine. "A state," it announced in words that Waite would have approved, "is free to adopt whatever economic policy may reasonably be deemed to promote public welfare, and to enforce that policy by legislation adapted to its purpose." Three years later in the case of *NLRB v. Jones and Laughlin Steel Corporation,* when the justices began the process of upholding the economic regulation of the New Deal, the permissive spirit of Waite's *Munn* opinion again triumphed.

Munn v. Illinois, of course, also had a more contemporary impact. The proprietors of the city's grain elevators, the Chicago *Tribune* reported a few days after the Supreme Court's decision, "are thoroughly reconstructed. They bow to the inevitable." They lowered their rates and began co-operating fully with the state's Railroad and Warehouse Commission. Two decades of arrogance by the warehousemen had come to an end; not only were their opponents politically dominant, but the elevator men found their monopolistic power weakened. They faced strong competition from new grain centers at Milwaukee and Minneapolis, and in addition, improved rail connections now permitted farmers to ship grain through Chicago to the East without temporarily storing it.

The railroads also bowed, although many of the midwestern states, responding to powerful railroad lobbies, later repealed or drastically loosened their regulatory laws. Illinois, however, remained a leader in strong railroad regulation; the farmers' influence prevented the repeal of the laws, which were sustained by both state and federal courts.

By 1877 the Patrons of Husbandry, who had provided much of the political support behind the regulatory laws, were but a shadow of their onetime strength. Internal dissensions and the financial collapse of its co-operative enterprises sharply reduced the organization's membership and destroyed its political influence. In fact, the Grange gradually reverted to its original social purposes and is today a thriving fraternal order. As for the unsavory firm of Munn & Scott, it too was no longer a factor by 1877, for it had passed out of existence.

But ultimately more significant than the immediate results and the conflicting motives of the many participants was the constitutional residue left by the struggles of the seventies: the clear announcement that legislatures might regulate business on behalf of the public interest, a principle that received additional vitality from Chief Justice Waite's assertion that the Court should be reluctant to upset regulatory laws passed by elected representatives. This was the meaning of *Munn v. Illinois,* and it provided a leading precedent for the day when American big business would find itself under continuing government regulation.

Dr. Magrath, a specialist in constitutional history, teaches political science at Brown University. His biography of the Chief Justice in the case of Munn v. Illinois, Morrison R. Waite: The Triumph of Character, *was published last year by Macmillan.*

For further reading: The Granger Movement, *by Solon J. Buck (University of Nebraska, 1963).*

Mason & Dixon: their Line and its Legend

CONTINUED FROM PAGE 29

and a call on Governor Sharpe at Annapolis. By late March, they were back at Captain Shelby's and again moving westward until, on June 16, Mason noted that they had reached "the most westernmost Waters [the headwaters of the Potomac] that runs to the Eastward in these parts." It seems, in fact, that the surveyors believed they were getting close to "the Boundary between the Natives and strangers, in these parts of His Brittanic Majesties Collonies."

The party now set itself to the task of establishing the actual markers for the border they had fixed. Mason noted in his journal on June 18, 1766:

Set a Post (18 inches square 3 feet in the Ground and 5 out) . . . mark'd M on ye South Side, P on ye North Side, and W on the West: and began to cut a Visto in the true Parallel, or Line between Maryland and Pennsylvania . . . By drawing it thro' Points, laid off from the Line we had run . . . toward the Post mark'd West in Mr. Bryan's field.

On the tangent line of the boundary between Maryland and the Delaware counties, the party was provided with limestone markers which had been cut in England for the purpose and shipped directly to various points on Chesapeake Bay. These were set at every mile point, with every fifth marker distinguished by a "crown stone" on which were carved the arms of the proprietors in place of the M or P. On one occasion while setting the stones along the "West Line" the scientists had an opportunity to view it from the summit of a hill and observe its curvature. Mason wrote, "I saw the Line, still form'd the arch of a . . . circle, very beautiful, and agreeable to the Laws of a Sphere." He also indulged his keen interest in landmarks along the way, and in recording the moral which might be drawn from them:

Went to see Fort Cumberland [he wrote on June 27, 1766] . . . Going to the Fort, I fell in to General Braddock's Road, which he cut thro' the Mountains to lead the Army under his command to the westward in the year 1755 but, fate: how hard: made thro' the desert a path, himself to pass; and never, never to return.

Most of the summer and autumn of 1766 was spent in prolonging the Maryland-Pennsylvania border to the approximate limit indicated by the Pennsylvania charter, five degrees in longitude westward from their starting point. The scientists also extended the line from the "Post marked West in Mr. Bryan's Field" eastward to the Delaware River. This project they completed on December 1, 1766. The commissioners, how-

ever, desired to have the main line go farther westward, and advised Mason and Dixon that Sir William Johnson, the royal agent for Indian affairs, was negotiating with the natives for its further extension into their territory. Additional work would await the outcome.

This was agreeable with Mason and Dixon. They had observed that the smooth terrain on what is now the Delmarva Peninsula was well adapted to a geodetic determination of the exact linear measure of one degree of latitude this far from the equator. They appealed to Maskelyne, then the Astronomer Royal at Greenwich, who arranged for the Royal Society to sponsor and finance the undertaking. The Society also granted their requested fee of £200 for the work, and assured them that if the proprietors should not be willing to give them their passage money after the delay which would be occasioned by this extra project, the Society would make it good.

But both Frederick, Lord Baltimore, and the Penns acquiesced in this research, and the Penns even sent the scientists some instruments which they had recently acquired. Not only would the work occupy the geodesists during the winter while negotiations between Sir William and the Indians were being carried on, but, as it developed later, the commissioners were interested in having the results of the investigation in order to fix the precise length of a degree of longitude along the east-west border. (This could be calculated from the value of a degree of latitude.)

Maskelyne sent his colleagues a long letter of instruction for the most accurate astronomical measurements, and through the instrument maker John Bird he arranged for the fashioning of a five-foot brass rod as a standard measure. With the aid of these and other improved instruments sent from abroad, Mason and Dixon determined, on the Delmarva Peninsula, the first precise value of dimensions of the earth ever made in North America.

In June, 1767, Sir William Johnson advised that the Six Nations had reluctantly consented to a limited extension of the border between Pennsylvania and Maryland. The situation could be rather delicate, the commissioners warned Mason and Dixon: "As the public Peace and your own Security may greatly depend on the Good Usage and Kind Treatment of these [Indian] Deputies" who were to accompany the party, "Spiritous Liquors" were to be given to them only in small quantities and not more than three times a day.

The Englishmen were eager to gather information

about the country beyond the Atlantic seaboard for scientific and perhaps for political reasons. Much of Mason's journal for this part of the survey was devoted to "a description of the Ohio and Mississippi, as describ'd to me by Mr. Hugh Crawford, our Interpreter, who has traversed these parts for 28 years." From this description he noted:

From the end of our line to the Ohio on a West Course is about forty miles . . . This West Line . . . if extended would . . . pass through the Southern part of the Illinois. The distance about 7 or 800 miles. A country says my informer thro' which you may travel 100 Miles, and not find one Hill, or one Acre of barren land.

The survey itself was not destined to go much farther. Shawnee war parties were reported to be active, and the escorting Senecas and Delawares had no intention of running into them. A sizable group of Indians had made up the escort, but throughout August and September there was a steady flow of departures. Mason and Dixon prevailed upon their axemen to stay with them, however, until on October 9, 1767, they reached the mouth of Dunkard Creek about thirty miles east of what is now Pennsylvania's southwest corner. Here the remaining Indians unanimously declared that the line could not be extended farther. The Englishmen accordingly took their final observations—"233 Miles, 3 Chains and 38 Links from the Post mark'd West."

Winter came early in the high altitudes, and as Mason and Dixon worked their way back eastward, foot-deep snow hampered them. It was not possible to convey the remaining limestone markers to the western-

---

A Short Time Between Drinks

Other colonial surveys besides that of Mason and Dixon were fraught with political overtones, both foreign and domestic. In 1726, for example, when North Carolina became a royal colony, the Crown directed its governor and that of Virginia to undertake a joint survey of the "dividing line." The colorful William Byrd II, Virginia's commissioner, tried to put the North Carolinians in a duly cooperative mood with his letter advising them of the plan the Virginians proposed to follow:

"It is very proper to acquaint you in what manner we intend to come provided, that so you Gentlemen, who are appointed in this same station, may if you please do the same honor to Your government. We shall have a Tent with us and a Marquis [canopy] for the convenience of ourselves and our servants. We shall be provided with as much Wine and Rum as will enable us and our men to drink every Night to the Success of the following Day, and because we understand there are many Gentiles on your frontier who never had an opportunity of being Baptised we shall have a Chaplain to make them Christians. For this Purpose we intend to rest in our Camp every Sunday that there may be leisure for so good a work. And whosoever of your Province shall be desirous of novelty may report on Sundays to our Tent and hear a Sermon. Of this you may please give Public Notice that the Charitable Intentions of this Government may meet with the happier Success."

After frequent delays and adventures—Byrd complained of the "anguish distempers" of the Dismal Swamp and of the "Adamites, without innocence," who lived with Indian women thereabout—the joint commission started westward. From the Atlantic to the foothills of the mountains, things went fairly well, but on Sunday, October 6, 1729, the North Carolina commissioners advised their Virginia colleagues that they did not intend to proceed farther. Byrd says the going was becoming rougher, and the Carolinians had failed to provide for an adequate flow of supplies to the advance bases. In any case, he reported this denouement of the joint project:

William Byrd II

"When the Divine Service was over, the Surveyors set about making the Plats of so much of the Line as we had run . . . Our pious Friends of Carolina assisted in this work with some Seeming Scruples, pretending it was a Violation of the Sabbath, which we were the more Surpriz'd at, because it happen'd to be the first Qualms of Conscience they had ever been troubled with during the whole journey. They had made no Bones of Staying from Prayers to hammer out an unnecessary Protest, tho' Divine Service was no Sooner over, but an unusual Fit of Godliness made them fancy that finishing the plats, which was now matter of necessity, was a prophanation of the Day. However, the Expediency of losing no time, for us who thought it our duty to finish what we had undertaken, made such a Labour pardonnable.

"In the Afternoon Mr. FitzWilliam, one of the Commissioners for Virginia, acquainted his Colleagues it was his Opinion, that by his Majesty's Order they could not proceed farther on the Line, but in Conjunction with the Commissioners of Carolina; for which reason he intended to retire, the Next Morning, with those Gentlemen.

"This looked a little odd in our Brother Commissioner [FitzWilliam, Byrd said, wanted to return to preside over the opening of court in Williamsburg and thus draw double pay as a judge and a Commissioner]; tho', in justice to Him, as well as to our Carolina Friends, they stuck by us as long as our good Liquor lasted, and were so kind to us as to drink our good Journey to the Mountains in the last Bottle we had left."

most part of the line, so mounds of earth and rocks were constructed to identify the border. By the end of December they were able to report to the joint commission that the work had been completed. The final request of the commission was that Mason and Dixon prepare a map of the border for an engraver and that they provide the commission with the length of a degree of longitude along the "West Line." The map was completed within a few weeks. As for the longitude measurement, Mason and Dixon reported with proper scientific qualification:

By comparing our measuration of a Degree of the Meridian with that made under the Arctic Circle, supposing the Earth to be a Spheroid of an uniform Density: a Degree of Longitude in the Parallel of the West Line is 53.5549 Miles. But as the Earth is not known to be exactly a Spheroid, nor whether it is everywhere of equal Density, and our own Experiment being not yet finish'd; we do not give in this as accurate. [The modern value is 53.2773 statute miles.]

It was accurate enough to satisfy the commissioners, who indeed pronounced themselves highly gratified with the entire project. From England the Penns took pains to send Mason and Dixon a letter of appreciation. Mason himself was elected to membership in the American Philosophical Society—quite possibly through the suggestion of Benjamin Franklin.

Although the survey ended the Pennsylvania-Maryland-Delaware border dispute, the original charter prepared for George Calvert, first Lord Baltimore, continued to play tricks. This document had put the western limits for Maryland at "the first fountains of the Pattowmack," but the Potomac River has so many forks and branches that unanimity of opinion could hardly be expected as to just what point was represented by this specification. The Mason-Dixon survey actually ran about thirty miles west of what was finally fixed by the United States Supreme Court, in 1912, as the northwest corner of Maryland. And so, as it turned out, the Calverts had paid half of the cost of a portion of the survey which had no bearing on their territory. For both proprietors it was an expensive undertaking, costing in all the equivalent of at least $100,000 in modern currency.

On September 11, 1768, four years and ten months after their arrival, the English geodesists sailed from New York for Falmouth. In London, on November 11, they submitted a final bill for £3,512/9 s., including passage money. Both proprietors willingly paid. In August, they already had joined in a petition to the King in Council to ratify the settlement of the border along the line surveyed. The royal ratification had no legal effect, but both sides seemed to feel that a seal of approval had been placed on the whole.

The daily progress of the survey had been recorded in a set of field notes kept by Mason, from which a final report was made to the commissioners. This journal was almost lost to posterity. Following the preparation of the "fair copies" of the field data for deposit with the two proprietaries, Mason or his descendants either lost or discarded the original manuscript. In 1860 it turned up in Halifax, Nova Scotia, among a pile of papers consigned to a trash heap. It was included among the Canadian exhibits at the Philadelphia Centennial in 1876, where it was called to the attention of Hamilton Fish, Secretary of State. After a brief negotiation with its owner, Judge Alexander James of the Supreme Court of Nova Scotia, the State Department purchased it for five hundred dollars in gold. It is now on file in the National Archives.

Jeremiah Dixon, always the lesser-known partner in the survey and other joint ventures with Mason, soon dropped out of history. He died in 1779. Charles Mason, for all his accomplishments as a scientist, fell into financial and physical decline in the early 1780's. In the fifteen years following the project in the New World, he had completed his star charts, which were to become a standard navigation aid, and had made various scientific expeditions for the Royal Society. Also, during this time, he assumed the responsibilities of a wife and family. But the remuneration for what was primarily a scholarly career was then, as now, inadequate for the demands of a growing household and declining health. Late in 1786 Mason turned up in Philadelphia with his wife and eight children. What prompted this return to the scene of his definitive project of twenty years earlier can only be conjectured. Apparently he had some hope that Franklin might be able to find a place for him. He may have thought of participating in the survey of western lands now opening up; but he died a few weeks after his arrival.

With the years, much of the work of the surveyors inevitably became undone. Some of the original boundary stones were removed, either by builders who found them handy for incorporating into a wall, or by farmers who found them in the way while plowing, or occasionally by someone who felt that his property was on the wrong side of the state line. In the western region, where earthen mounds had formed the markers, the elements tended to obliterate them. The first of several resurveys was begun in 1849 to re-establish the complex boundary relations at the northwest corner of Delaware. More refined instruments and more accurate astronomical and geodetic data for the mathematical evaluation of observations disclosed slight errors in the work of Mason and Dixon, but Lieutenant Colonel James D. Graham of the U.S.

Army Engineers, who supervised the 1849 resurvey, made a point of praising "the surprising accuracy" of the 1764 observations. Colonel Graham's reaction was to be echoed in 1885, when the U.S. Coast and Geodetic Survey confirmed the western extension of the line which divided Pennsylvania from what had become, in the meantime, West Virginia.

Another resurvey was run in 1902—again under joint commissions from Maryland and Pennsylvania and with the aid of the U.S. Coast and Geodetic Survey. Where practicable, the original markers were reset in concrete; otherwise, new stones were put in place with the dates 1766/7 and 1902 carved, respectively, on their eastern and western faces. The result, stated the commissioners in their final report, was to confirm the remarkably small degree of error in the work of Mason and Dixon, which was carried on through wild country without the benefit of modern instruments. For the two English scientists who laid down the line, this should be a sufficient memorial.

A. Hughlett Mason—no kin of Charles—has recently retired as senior physicist for the Army Chief of Staff. William F. Swindler, professor of legal history at the College of William and Mary, is a specialist in constitutional law and American political history.

The Enigma of General Howe

CONTINUED FROM PAGE 11

which they hoped would satisfy both the truculent King and his supporters as well as the opposition. They decided to appoint Vice Admiral Lord Richard Howe naval commander in North America, with the dual title of "peace commissioner."

Lord Howe was far more reluctant than his brother to take a military command, and his negotiations with his own government are another revealing instance of the family's thinking. The Admiral insisted that his brother be included as another peace commissioner, and he initially hoped the commission would be given broad powers of negotiation. But George III's attitude toward the colonies soon left Admiral Howe with little more than the power to grant pardons, while he was ordered to assert Parliament's right to tax, to demand payment for losses sustained by Loyalists, and to "correct and reform" colonial governments.

At one point, Howe almost resigned in disgust; the King agreed that he ought to do so, for the good of the service. But George's prime minister, Lord North, was as anxious as the Howes to reach an accommodation with America. North finally persuaded the Admiral to accept his commission and to rely for the success of his mission upon his personal charm and wide friendship with American leaders.

There is some evidence of a considerable gap between the King's punitive written instructions and the verbal assurances Howe received from the Ministry. When he came home in 1778, the Admiral declared in Parliament that everyone knew he and the administration had an affair to settle. But an even more compelling motive for Howe's acceptance of the enfeebled "peace commission" was his brother's assignment to put down the rebellion. As the leader of the family, Lord Howe had almost certainly advised William to accept his general's commission, which he could not resign now without being called coward, even traitor.

General William Howe, meanwhile, had retreated somewhat ignominiously from Boston on March 17, his departure hurried by the appearance of Washington's cannon on Dorchester Heights (see "Big Guns for Washington" in the April, 1955, AMERICAN HERITAGE). During his nine months in the city, the General's only triumph was the acquisition of blonde and beautiful Mrs. Joshua Loring as his mistress. Much has been made of this liaison, which continued throughout Howe's American campaigns. Judge Thomas Jones, the Loyalist historian, compared Howe to Mark Antony, declaring Sir William sacrificed an empire for the charms of his Boston Cleopatra. A mistress was hardly remarkable among eighteenth-century English aristocrats, shocking though she may have been to pious Americans, and there is not an iota of evidence that Mrs. Loring ever had the slightest influence on Howe's policies.

The General evacuated his forces from Boston, regrouped and refitted his regiments at Halifax, and joined his brother on Staten Island in the summer of 1776. Admiral Howe brought massive reinforcements of German mercenaries and English regulars, swelling the army to 32,000 men. Washington, against his better judgment, was committed to defend New York against this host with less than 20,000 soldiers, most of them untrained.

The Battle of Long Island was Howe's first exhibition of his talents as Commander in Chief. On August 27, 1776, attacking Americans entrenched in the commanding Brooklyn hills, Howe faked a frontal assault with half his army and after an all-night flanking march swept in upon his astonished enemies from the rear. In an hour the affair had turned into a total rout, with redcoats and Hessians hunting demoralized Americans through the woods like rabbits. Three generals, three colonels, four lieutenant colonels, three majors, eighteen captains, forty-three lieutenants, and more than one thousand enlisted men were captured.

What was left of the trapped American regiments fell back to redoubts on Brooklyn Heights. The British and Germans, flushed with triumph and scarcely damaged (total British casualties were less than 400), surged forward to smash this last barrier between themselves and total victory. Behind the ramparts, Washington and some 9,000 badly shaken Americans awaited the inevitable assault. But as the redcoats exchanged opening fusillades of musketry with the defenders, orders came from the British rear to cease and desist.

Major General John Vaughan, who was in command of a column of Grenadiers, was astonished, and sent back word that he could easily carry the redoubts, with little loss. But again the order arrived from General Howe to fall back, for "the troops had done handsomely enough." Howe later explained that he did this because he saw that the American defenses could be had at "a cheap price" by "regular approaches." In other words, siege techniques. This was certainly in accord with the standard eighteenth-century mode of making war. Armies were small and soldiers were precious (especially to Howe, who was 3,000 miles from any reinforcements). But Washington made this caution look foolish by shipping his entire army back to Manhattan two nights later.

The Howes were now in complete control of Staten Island, Long Island, and the waters surrounding Manhattan. The Americans did not have so much as a gunboat to oppose the immense fleet Lord Howe had brought with him. Even before the Battle of Long Island, two British warships had run the supposedly impregnable American shore batteries along the Hudson and anchored near Kingsbridge. From a military point of view, Washington was in a bag; all Howe had to do was land above Manhattan and draw the string.

Moreover, the rout on Long Island had shattered American morale. "The country is struck with panic," Nathanael Greene wrote to Washington, who himself reported to Congress that the defeat had "dispirited too great a proportion of our troops and filled their minds with apprehension and dispair. The militia are dismayed, intractable and impatient. . . . Great numbers of them have gone off; in some instances, almost by whole regiments." If Howe had struck hard and swiftly, it is difficult to believe that the American army could have survived.

Instead, the Howes spent the next two weeks as peace commissioners. Six weeks before, Lord Howe had sent a letter to Washington himself proposing a parley as a "means of preventing the further effusion of Blood" and arranging "Peace and lasting union between Great Britain and America." Foolishly, he had addressed it to "George Washington Esqr," thus ignoring the belligerent status of the Americans which the use of Washington's military title would have implied. They were, the address inferred, merely traitorous subjects of the Crown who upon capture might be hanged. After a conference with his officers, Washington refused to accept the letter. Now the Howes tried again. Captured General John Sullivan was sent to Philadelphia with flowery words about an accommodation, and Congress grudgingly decided to send Benjamin Franklin, John Adams, and Edward Rutledge to see what the Howes had to say. It soon became apparent that the only power they had was to grant pardons, and the Americans refused to admit that they had done anything to warrant pardons. The conference quickly foundered.

The fruitless peace talks gave the Americans time to hail Washington's retreat from Long Island as proof of his military genius, and generally stiffen their backs for the defense of Manhattan. Although Washington drew a large portion of his army back to the northern end of the island, lest Howe attempt the obvious maneuver of a landing above his lines, the American general left over 5,000 men under Israel Putnam at the lower end, and even his more withdrawn brigades would have been helpless against a sudden move by water, under cover of darkness. Washington had never before commanded more than a regiment in battle—Boston had been only a siege—and his conduct reveals the indecisive thinking of the learner.

But Howe did not land above the lines. On September 15, he sent his men ashore at Kip's Bay, where today Thirty-fourth Street meets the East River. Troyer Steele Anderson, perhaps the best of the Howe historians, argues that not even the two weeks of peace maneuvers were really a delay, because Howe had to wait that long anyway for tides which permitted him to move his small assault boats up the Brooklyn shore by night. But this does not explain his failure to land above Manhattan and trap Washington, as the exasperated Henry Clinton begged him to do.

The Kip's Bay landing was another rout for the Americans. The raw militia fled at the first barrage from the covering warships, and the regulars surged ashore without losing a man. A determined thrust across Manhattan might have trapped Putnam and his 5,000 defenders, most of them still at the tip of the island, but once more Howe was satisfied with the first chase, and let the real game get away. Harassed by their commander and his aides, one of whom was a twenty-year-old major named Aaron Burr, Putnam's men quick-marched up the western edge of Manhattan and rejoined the main body on Harlem Heights. The same caution Howe had displayed at Long Island is an equally valid explanation, of course. He was conducting an amphibious landing, and his first thought was to consolidate his beachhead. Throughout his narrative before the House of Commons, Howe repeatedly emphasized caution as his first principle. He had, he said, labored constantly to hold down casualties and avoid a "check" which would give the rebels a chance to declare a victory.

A general who makes caution his byword can always point to disasters which might have happened if rash risks and undue haste had been his army's policy. But more than one person has been puzzled by this sudden, passionate fondness for caution on Howe's part, when all of his previous military career had exhibited a love of the long chance and the hair-raising gamble.

For a full month after his seizure of New York, Howe allowed Washington to sit on Harlem Heights practically unmolested, while the British troops were set to digging defensive fortifications. Looking back at it now, the situation seems almost comic. A great army of well-trained professionals, superbly equipped and supported by an unopposed fleet, has just routed its untrained enemy twice. Then what does the victorious general do? Go on the defensive! True, the skirmish called "the Battle of Harlem Heights" showed the Americans had some sting left. But that was little more than a brush between advance guards. Every evidence pointed to the inability of Washington to stand firm had Howe struck a massive blow.

Howe solemnly told the House of Commons it would have cost him 1,000 to 1,500 men to storm Harlem Heights, in his opinion an excessive price. But he had a more difficult time explaining why he wasted a month of the best campaigning weather sitting on lower Manhattan staring up at Washington. He said he was short of horses; furthermore, none of the inhabitants of America was able to give him a "military description" of the terrain across which he would have to advance if he landed north of the American army.

This terrain was Westchester County, a region which abounded in Loyalists willing to serve Howe as guides and map makers. Even had that not been so, Howe's excuse would still have earned ridicule. Bellamy Partridge, author of *Sir Billy Howe*, wrote: "Two weeks to find a short cut across from the Sound to the Hudson River! A matter of from five to eight miles! Washington would have run a survey across there in two days; and in two weeks he could have made a topographical map of the district, with altitudes and the depth of all watercourses plainly indicated, in addition to the roads and

clearings and favorable locations for combat."

Nevertheless, when Howe finally decided to move, he did so masterfully. At three A.M. on October 12 he put his soldiers aboard his brother's ships and slipped silently up the East River and through Hell Gate in a thick fog. But once they reached Long Island Sound, this know-how abruptly vanished. They landed the troops on Throg's Neck, a marshy point of land that was virtually an island at high water; twenty-five American riflemen concealed behind a woodpile were able to prevent their advance. Howe then went into camp, and spent six days on the Neck, while baggage and supplies were brought up from New York. Meanwhile, Washington was frantically evacuating his cumbersome column of 13,000 men from Harlem Heights over Kingsbridge, his one avenue of escape into Westchester. Shortages of wagons and horses reduced him to a crawl. The artillery had to be dragged by hand. In one of his worst military blunders, Washington left 2,800 men behind to hold Fort Washington, on the New York side of the Hudson, and another garrison at Fort Lee, on the Jersey shore opposite, both under the command of Nathanael Greene.

In a single night, Howe put all his men back aboard his ships and landed them at Pell's Point, in present-day Pelham. He met some initial resistance from about 750 New Englanders under Colonel John Glover of Marblehead, but they soon fell back toward the main American army. Only six miles away, down a straight road which any Tory in Westchester would have been happy to show Howe on a map, the American army was still straggling across Kingsbridge in a long, exposed, disorganized line. Even the ardently pro-American historian Christopher Ward admits that if Howe had attacked "there could hardly have been any other result than a complete rout." But Howe spent three days in New Rochelle, and then marched to Mamaroneck, where he spent another four days.

A rapid march to White Plains by Howe's 4,000 light infantry could have seized the high ground around the village and pinned Washington and his army against the Hudson River. Instead, Howe let Washington do the seizing, and when the British arrived at White Plains they found the Americans blocking their path. Howe was forced to fight, after he had seemingly done everything he could to maneuver Washington out of New York without a battle.

At White Plains the armies were almost equal in size, and Washington had the advantage of choosing the field. But Howe's first move, on October 28, unhinged the whole American position. He sent 4,000 men against Chatterton's Hill, and after fierce resistance from entrenched Americans he threw in his cavalry, which totally demolished two regiments of rebel militia and forced the rest of the defenders to quit the hill. Chatterton's gave Howe a position from which he could outflank the rest of Washington's army. Moreover, Howe now lay between the Fort Washington garrison and the main army. It was the dream of every general. He was in a position to devour both American forces at his leisure.

But once again Howe dallied, while at White Plains Washington frantically threw up flimsy redoubts made of cornstalks from nearby fields, with earth clinging to their roots. Reinforced by two brigades from Manhattan, Howe now had 20,000 men. "A brisk drive," Bellamy Partridge says, "would have scattered the patriots into the hills." Another defeat probably would have destroyed Washington's already dwindling military reputation. But Howe never made the climactic assault. During three days of inaction, he let Washington withdraw the bulk of his army northward to a stronger position at North Castle, and then, on November 4, the entire British army turned around and went clanking off to New York without firing another shot.

When asked why he had not pressed the attack at White Plains, Howe blandly told the House of Commons: "An assault upon the enemy's right which was opposed to the Hessian troops, was intended. The committee must give me credit when I assure them that I have political reasons, and no other for declining to explain why that assault was not made."

Some historians argue that Howe had received the plans of Fort Washington from a Tory spy, and seeing that he could take this pseudo-stronghold with ease, he decided to make that his final battle of the campaign season, then drawing to a close. If this thesis is true, then the "political reasons" would have been a desire to protect the Tory spy from the revengeful Americans. It is a feeble argument. In the first place, Fort Washington would still have been there after Howe had smashed Washington's army at White Plains. He could have scooped it up as an afterthought on his triumphant journey back to Manhattan. In the second place, why didn't Howe, who used fairly plain English in the rest of his narrative, say something about this spy, without revealing his name? "Political reasons" suggest something far larger—even a policy that was guiding Howe's military conduct.

Howe did in fact capture Fort Washington, bagging 2,837 prisoners in a brilliant multipronged assault on November 15. Washington, meanwhile, again divided his army, carrying 5,400 men into New Jersey and leaving the rest to guard the Hudson. Only the violent entreaties of Lord Cornwallis persuaded Howe to pursue him. The American catastrophe at Fort Washington was almost repeated at Fort Lee, when Cornwallis led 4,000 picked troops across the Hudson and landed

The King's Cousins

George Augustus Howe   Richard Howe

There were originally three Howe brothers, all Whigs, all distinguished in arms, all in turn holders of a viscountcy in the Irish peerage. Like the Scottish peerage today, the Irish one merely elected a few of their number to sit in the Lords at Westminster; the remainder were free to run for the British House of Commons. Of this convenience all three Howes availed themselves. Brigadier General George Augustus Howe, Third Viscount, the democratic and well-beloved eldest brother who fell at Ticonderoga in 1758, had been Member for Nottingham. That borough at once elected his youngest brother, William, in his place. The middle brother, Richard, inherited the title as Fourth Viscount Howe (and was hence addressed as "Lord Howe"); he was also elected to the Commons for Dartmouth, and both surviving brothers remained M.P.'s through the Revolution. (For a parallel, imagine both Admiral Halsey and, say, General Eisenhower also serving as congressmen during the last war.) There was also a sister, Lady Howe, who had known and played chess with Benjamin Franklin, as the romanticized old engraving below shows; she was briefly involved in the peace-making efforts of the family.

It did the Howes no harm socially, to put it mildly, that their father, a former governor of Barbados, had married the daughter of the plump Baroness Kilmansegge, one of the German mistresses of George I; they were thus cousins by the left hand to King George III himself. Yet the Howes had genuine ability of their own. William won his own knighthood. Richard, "Black Dick" to an admiring fleet, led the bold relief of Gibraltar in 1782 and smashed the navy of Revolutionary France at the battle called "The Glorious First of June" in 1794. He died an earl, full of honors, in 1799; the Irish viscountcy passed to Sir William, who also had no sons, expiring with that enigmatic soldier in 1814.

above the redoubts at dawn. Frantic haste on the part of Nathanael Greene got his men out of the place, with nothing but their muskets. Their blankets, a thousand barrels of flour, 400,000 cartridges, and dozens of precious cannon had to be left behind.

Washington was now being pursued by a general who had none of Howe's tendency to dally. While the American army, disheartened by the loss of Fort Washington, melted away, Cornwallis hounded the remainder across New Jersey. Entering Newark as Washington's rear guard went out the other end of the town, he pushed his troops twenty miles in a single day through a driving rainstorm, trying to catch Washington at New Brunswick before he forded the Raritan.

On December 1 Washington got his last man across the river as Cornwallis' advance guard came up. The armies were within cannon shot of each other, and the river was "in a variety of places, knee deep only," according to eyewitnesses. There was nothing to stop Cornwallis from charging across and falling on Washington's dispirited remnant of an army, now barely 3,000 strong. Instead, the British sat down on the wrong side of the river, and did not move for four days. Orders from William Howe had arrived, forbidding them to advance until he had brought up "reinforcements."

Again, caution perfectly explains such a decision. But when Howe arrived he brought only a single brigade, and they proceeded to move forward at a more familiar pace, giving Washington time to get his rear guard across the Delaware at Trenton just as the British advance guard reached the river bank. Charles Stedman, the British historian who was an officer in Howe's army, says with dry sarcasm: "General Howe appeared to have calculated with the greatest accuracy the exact time necessary for the enemy to make his escape."

Washington had collected every available boat for seventy miles along the river, and drawn them to the other side. This supposedly stymied Howe. But there was a well-stocked lumber yard in Trenton, and four blacksmith shops. If Howe had wanted to cross the river, he could have built himself a small fleet in a week. There were no fewer than nine ferry landings for Washington to guard. The rebel capital of Philadelphia, already in panic, lay within a day's march.

But Howe had no immediate interest in Philadelphia. Nor was he interested in destroying Washington. He only wanted to drive him out of New Jersey, so that he could get down to the business of restoring that territory to loyalty and order. He issued a proclamation offering pardon and the enjoyment of liberty and property rights to all who would sign a declaration of loyalty within sixty days. Even those who had fought in Washington's army were included. New Jersey responded, almost en masse. To guarantee continued tranquillity, Howe established a series of strong cantonments along the Delaware, most of them manned by Hessians who had fought brilliantly at Fort Washington a month before.

It was now mid-December, true, and Howe, like almost all military commanders of that era, was anxious to get his troops into winter quarters. But was this excuse enough to discard total victory when he had it within his grasp? The answer would seem to be that Howe did not see total victory in military terms as the key to his policy. What he and his brother were aiming at, from the start, was peace by reconciliation. To achieve this they had to balance American extremists, who insisted on independence, against extremists of the opposite persuasion back home, who insisted on all-out repression. If they annihilated Washington and his army and captured the Congress, what would there be left to reconcile? The British extremists could be held in check only by making sure there was still an American force in being with whom to negotiate. The American extremists, on the other hand, had to be shown that they had no hope of winning independence against the might of Great Britain, and that to carry the rebellion further was folly. What better way to do this than to thrash the Americans repeatedly and drive them out of selected colonies, which could then be pacified and held up to the rest of the country as examples of British benevolence?

Howe's letters to Lord Germain indicate this thinking. On September 25, before the fiasco at White Plains, he was writing: "I have not the smallest prospect of finishing the contest this campaign, not until the Rebels see preparations in the spring, *that may preclude all thoughts of further resistance* [author's

Howe's point of attack at White Plains, on October 28, 1776, was Chatterton's Hill, where his dragoons, in the war's first formal cavalry charge, routed an inexperienced force of New York and Connecticut militia. But again he failed to pursue his advantage, and again George Washington slipped away.

italics]. To this end, I would propose eight or ten line of battle ships, with a number of supernumerary seamen for manning boats . . . We must also have recruits from Europe, not finding the Americans disposed to serve with arms, notwithstanding the hopes held out to me on my arrival at this port."

On November 30, Howe spelled out to Germain his plan for the next campaign. It was ambitious. An offensive army of 10,000 would move from Providence, Rhode Island, toward Boston; another army of 10,000 would move up the Hudson River to Albany, leaving 5,000 men to defend New York; finally, a defensive army of 8,000 men would cover New Jersey and pose a threat to Philadelphia, which Howe proposed to attack in the autumn. With the New England and middle colonies thus subdued, Howe planned to finish the rebellion in the winter by moving into Virginia and the Carolinas. Again, the phrasing of his letter is significant. "Were . . . the force I have mentioned sent out, it *would strike such terror throughout the country* that little resistance would be made to the progress of his Majesty's arms." Once more, Howe is thinking in terms of discouraging the rebels, rather than of defeating them in the field.

To make his new plans work, Howe asked for 15,000 more men. He was turned down. Further, Washington and his little army proved unwilling to roll over and play dead: striking through the sleet at Trenton on Christmas night, they captured almost the entire 1,400-man garrison of Hessians. The victory restored the patriots' sinking morale. Howe at first called it a "misfortune," but a few weeks later, he was writing what is perhaps his most revealing letter to Germain:

It is with much concern that I am to inform your Lordship the unfortunate and untimely defeat at Trenton has thrown us further back, than was at first apprehended, from the great encouragement given to the rebels.

I do not now see a prospect of terminating the war but by a general action . . .

"I do not *now* see." Quite casually, perhaps without realizing it, Howe here admits that until Trenton, a "general action" was not included in his plan to end the war. Could this explain Washington's repeated escapes from disaster at Long Island, Manhattan, White Plains, and throughout New Jersey?

Washington's victory at Trenton could be attributed to the fortunes of war. But Germain's refusal to send reinforcements seemed to Howe a low blow, especially since a well-equipped army was handed to General John Burgoyne for a descent from Canada to Albany. Burgoyne had a scheme of his own for ending the war. At Albany he would join with a force under Howe proceeding up the Hudson, and with another from the west

under Barry St. Leger. If all went well, New England would be cut off from the rest of the colonies and the two halves of the infant nation could be conquered at will.

But a new note now enters Howe's thinking: resentment. From Howe's point of view, Burgoyne had stolen from him the soldiers he needed for the master plan he himself had proposed to Germain. Howe wrote to his lordship, telling him that the master plan would now have to be drastically altered. On April 1, 1777, he told Germain, "I propose to invade Pennsylvania by sea." He admitted this meant evacuating the Jerseys, and added with irony: "Restricted as I am from entering upon more extensive operations by the want of forces, my hopes of terminating the war this year are vanished."

Then, on April 5, Howe wrote to Guy Carleton, the British commander in Canada, telling him he had "but little expectation that I shall be able from the want of sufficient strength in the army to detach a corps in the beginning of the campaign to act up Hudson's River." Meanwhile, Germain in England wrote Howe approving his plan to invade Pennsylvania by sea. But at the same time he wrote to Carleton, assuring him he would write to Howe to "guarantee the most speedy junction of the two armies." Alas for the hopes and dreams of George III, Germain never sent such a letter. All Howe ever got was a copy of Germain's letter to Carleton, which nowhere contained a specific order limiting Howe to advancing up the Hudson River, and a paragraph in a later letter in which Germain, approving a modification of his Pennsylvania plan, trusted "it will be executed in time for you to co-operate with the army ordered to proceed from Canada." A major disaster was shaping up: "Gentleman Johnny" Burgoyne would be fighting his way to Albany to join up with Howe, who instead would be on his way to Philadelphia.

Co-operating with Burgoyne was the one thing Howe had no interest in doing. His defense of his decision to sail to Philadelphia pulsates with resentment in every line: "Had I adopted the plan to go up the Hudson River," he told the House of Commons, "it would have been alleged that I had wasted the campaign with a considerable army under my command, merely to ensure the progress of the northern army, which could have taken care of itself, provided I had made a diversion in its favour by drawing off to the southward the main army under General Washington. Would not my enemies have gone further, and insinuated that, alarmed at the rapid success which the honourable General [Burgoyne] had a right to expect when Ticonderoga fell, I had enviously grasped a share of the merit which would otherwise have been all his own? and let me add, would not Ministers have told you, as they truly might, that I had acted without any orders or instructions from them?"

Nevertheless, according to Clinton, Howe's plan to sail to Philadelphia and turn his back on Burgoyne (who was in no trouble at that moment, it must be admitted) appalled every man in the army except for Lord Cornwallis and Major General James Grant. Among his papers there is a memorandum Clinton wrote to a friend at the time: "By God these people can not mean what they give out, they must intend to go up Hudson's River & deceive us all, if they do I for one forgive."

But Howe did mean what he said: on July 23 he put his men aboard his brother's mighty fleet of 260 ships and set sail from Sandy Hook. Not even Washington could believe Sir William was going to desert Burgoyne, and for days the Americans were in a frenzy of uncertainty, distributing their army all over New Jersey so they could be ready to march north or south, depending on where Howe appeared. A week later, the Howes paused off the mouth of the Delaware. There, having been told that the Americans had blocked and fortified the river, they decided to bear away for the Chesapeake. Contrary winds and currents delayed them: not until August 14 did they enter the bay, and it took eleven days to reach Head of Elk, fifteen miles from New Castle, where the army disembarked.

Men and horses had suffered terribly from heat and from the shortage of fresh water. Almost all the animals had to be destroyed. And as the British historian Sir George Otto Trevelyan acidly points out, the net result of this incredible voyage was to place the British army ten miles farther from Philadelphia than it had been at Amboy, in New Jersey, the previous December.

Even so, Howe was to have one more opportunity to achieve total victory. At Brandywine Creek on September 11, Washington grimly accepted the challenge of a "general action" to save Philadelphia, but he permitted Howe to repeat the tactics by which he had won the Battle of Long Island. While the Hessians under Knyphausen made a mock frontal assault at Chad's Ford, Howe and Cornwallis swept around the American flank and appeared in the rear of John Sullivan's brigade. These men, the bulk of the American right wing, were strung out along a two-mile line running through dense woods. Sullivan had to draw them in and shift them at a right angle to their first position to confront Howe. It was a dubious maneuver with untrained troops; if Howe had attacked as soon as he reached Sullivan's rear, Sullivan and perhaps the rest of the American army would have retreated. But the British had been on the march since early morning,

and it was half past two. Howe ordered a halt for lunch. Such consideration was typical of Howe, and it was why his men loved him so much.

When the British attacked at three thirty, Sullivan's men were the first to break. But the center fought well, yielding ground stubbornly, and when Knyphausen attacked across the Ford, he met equally fierce resistance from Anthony Wayne. Still, by nightfall the terrific pressure exerted by the British had reduced the American army to almost total disorganization. Except for a few regiments under Greene, Christopher Ward tells us, "thousands of beaten men, already dispersed before the final retreat and now uncontrolled by any sort of military discipline, thronged the road in utter confusion." But Howe ordered no pursuit. His men were weary, and he let them spend the next day resting on the field. And on September 26 he reached his major objective, when Cornwallis entered the rebel capital with a force of British and Hessians.

Meanwhile, Burgoyne was meeting disaster in the wilderness. Surrounded by a militia army three times the size of his own, he surrendered at Saratoga on October 17. But even before Howe heard confirmation of this doleful news—in fact, on October 22, less than a month after he marched into Philadelphia—Sir William sent in his resignation. His actual words are again interesting: "From the little attention given to my recommendations since the commencement of my command, I am led to hope that I may be relieved from this very *painful* service, wherein I have not the good fortune to enjoy the necessary confidence and support of my superiors . . ."

As we have seen, there is considerable evidence that the service was "painful" to Sir William Howe from the day he arrived in America. His policy of peace by reconciliation had proved to be a will-o'-the-wisp. He was about to be crushed between Washington's stubborn belligerence and the growing impatience of the "hard line" ministers in the Royal government. When he went home to confront his enemies in the ministry, he stoutly defended his original goal. "For, Sir, although some persons condemn me for having endeavoured to conciliate His Majesty's rebellious subjects . . . instead of irritating them by a contrary mode of proceeding, yet am I, from many reasons, satisfied in my own mind that I acted in that particular for the benefit of the King's service. Ministers themselves, I am persuaded, did at one time entertain a similar doctrine . . ."

Not a minister rose to deny this statement. In fact it was the government, using its paid-up majority in Parliament, who hastily extinguished the Howe inquiry before it could reach any conclusion. Moreover, the government treated Howe with the greatest deference, handing him one well-paying sinecure after another until he died in 1814.

It seems clear that Sir William Howe was anything but a blunderer or a fool. Nor, though he enjoyed his bottle, his cards and the lady Loring, did he ever let them seriously interfere with what he set out to do in America. The mistake (perhaps, from a personal point of view, the tragedy) of Sir William Howe originated in the judgment of the King's vacillating ministers, who gave him the job in the first place. The great Swiss military writer Jomini sums it up as a violation of the art of war. "To commit the execution of a purpose to one who disapproves of the plan of it, is to employ but one third of the man; his heart and his head are against you; you have command only of his hands."

Thomas J. Fleming is the author of Now We Are Enemies: The Story of Bunker Hill, *and* Beat the Last Drum: The Siege of Yorktown, 1781.

For further reading: The American Heritage Book of the Revolution, *Narrative by Bruce Lancaster (American Heritage Publishing Company, 1958);* The War of the Revolution, *by Christopher Ward, Volume I (Macmillan, 1952).*

The Great White Fleet

CONTINUED FROM PAGE 34

narrow channel. Running in at night under fire from the enemy's ancient shore batteries, they sank the ship, but she went down lengthwise rather than athwart the channel, and the way remained open.

Next the Army tried to drive Cervera out. In the second half of June some 17,000 troops were landed at Daiquiri, about halfway between Santiago and the recently captured base at Guantanamo Bay. Fighting not only a well-entrenched, though hungry, enemy but heat and tropical disease, the outnumbered American army also failed. The commanding general called upon Admiral Sampson to dash through the enemy's minefields and collar the Spaniards; he refused. But Sampson was willing to talk the matter over. He was on his way to a conference with the general on Sunday, July 3, when Pasqual Cervera abruptly solved the matter.

Prodded from Madrid, the reluctant Spanish admiral headed out to sea—and provided the American Navy with another great morning. The Americans, led by Sampson's second-in-command, Commodore Schley, destroyed all of Cervera's ships without losing a single ship of their own; only one man was killed, a yeoman on the *Brooklyn*. When Admiral Sampson heard the gunfire, he turned the swift *New York* around and crowded on all speed, but he arrived too late. His report to Washington, "The fleet under my command offers the nation as a Fourth of July present the whole of Cervera's fleet . . . ," precipitated a bitter wrangle with Schley that went on for years.

Nonetheless there was glory enough for all. Everyone was gallant, officers shouted heroic phrases ("Don't cheer, boys, the poor devils are dying," cried Captain Jack Philip of the *Texas*), and the scene was bright with flying flags and flaming guns. After the battle the victors risked their lives to rescue their recent enemies from exploding ships, sharks, and Cuban guerrillas on the beach; captured Spanish officers were taken to Annapolis, where they were treated as gentlemen-heroes.

"A splendid little war," wrote an exultant John Hay from London, and most would agree. Cuba was free after four centuries of Spanish rule and now we had colonies of our own: Puerto Rico, Guam, and the Philippines. The Navy had become immensely popular. Congress provided for so many new ships that the nation's shipyards were clogged for years.

Not everyone, however, was as self-satisfied as Hay. Within the Navy serious questions arose about American strategy (splitting the Flying Squadron from the rest of the fleet), tactics (Santiago was a captains' battle with no direction from Commodore Schley), and gunnery (firing at ranges of a mile or two, only 1.3 per cent of the shots hit home). Perhaps the performance was no worse than anyone else's might have been. In any event it was better than the Spaniards', and that was enough for that war.

In September, 1901, Theodore Roosevelt, a political nonconformist whom Republican chieftains had tried to bury in the Vice Presidency, unexpectedly became President when William McKinley was assassinated. For the seven and a half years that Roosevelt was in the White House, the Navy toiled and prospered. Roosevelt was a zestful player at world power politics. He believed not only that "a great country must have a foreign policy," but also that "there is some nobler ideal for a great nation than being an assemblage of prosperous hucksters." The Navy became his chief means for executing his views on foreign policy.

Tiny gunboats commanded by officers fresh from Annapolis cruised, ready for battle, up and down the Philippines and far up the pirate-ridden rivers of China. Others roamed the Caribbean, prepared to

POURED BACK ABOARD

This 1887 engraving from *Harper's Weekly*, based on a drawing by Frederic Remington, is titled "The Last Aboard"—referring, of course, to the acrobatic fellow in the blue uniform and leg irons who is being gently assisted to the deck of a U.S. Navy man-of-war. Some siren song of the mainland has obviously smitten him—but a few days in the brig will cure all that. Commenting on this tableau, an anonymous *Harper's* moralist spoke of the "certain human tendencies" in sailors "which, for all that one can see, will last to the end of things nautical. . . . In the case of the sailor whose return is represented in the picture . . . the indisposition to resume the humdrum of a seafaring life is most marked. . . . His mates understand that he means no offence to them personally by being burdensome, and that his balky behavior is directed merely against the general system of ship discipline, which, on such an occasion particularly, seems very harsh and grinding to him.

"The types of sailors represented," the writer concluded, "are taken from Uncle Sam's navy, and may be seen in life just at present at the Brooklyn Navy-yard, where, though satisfactory results have attended the energetic temperance crusade conducted by the worthy chaplain of the *Vermont,* the backsliders are sufficiently numerous to supply many originals for the subject of our illustration."

Harper's Weekly, FEBRUARY 19, 1887

land marines and seamen on turbulent tropic shores.

In November, 1903, negotiations with Colombia for a ship canal through the Isthmus of Panama failed. Not long after, that province flared into revolt. When loyal troops arrived at Colón they found the U.S. gunboat *Nashville* in the harbor and her landing party ashore, effectively blocking the restoration of Colombian authority. Roosevelt quickly recognized Panama as an independent state, and soon had his canal site.

The gunboats may have borne the White Man's Burden, but they did so under cover of the big ships. Twice war seemed imminent: in 1901, with Germany, when it threatened to slice off a portion of Venezuela in payment for a bad debt, and again, in 1907, with Japan. Twice the President mobilized his battle fleet, and twice the war threat vanished.

During Roosevelt's administration, the American Navy became, for a time, the second most powerful in the world, boasting more than forty big armored ships—compared with seven during the war with Spain. Only England had more heavy ships (ninety-eight in 1908), while France came third with thirty-three; Germany had thirty-two, and Japan twenty-two. (Russia, long in third place, had been humiliated by the Japanese in 1904–05 and for many years would no longer be counted among the great sea powers.) Germany, Japan, and the United States were on their way up; indeed, after Roosevelt left office in 1909, Germany passed the United States. France was steadily losing ground.

Moreover, from 1905 on, for the first time in peace, most of the American battleships worked together in a single group. And, by previous standards, they were beginning to shoot with marvelous accuracy. While the fleet maneuvered east of Norfolk and south of Cuba, selected officers took graduate courses in strategy, tactics, and international law at the Naval War College in Newport, which Mahan had presided over in its precarious early years.

Then, toward the end of his second term, Roosevelt, always the master showman, came up with the most dramatic stroke of all. With the Japanese war problem still before him, he announced that he would send sixteen of his best battleships from the Atlantic to the Pacific in a show of strength. Dazzling in its white paint, the fleet sailed from Hampton Roads, Virginia, in December, 1907, with Rear Admiral Robley ("Fighting Bob") Evans leading in his flagship, the *Connecticut*. The first night out, Evans had a surprise for his 15,000 officers and men: ". . . after a short stay on the Pacific Coast, it is the President's intention to have the fleet return to the Atlantic Coast by way of the Mediterranean." They were going to steam around the world. The voyage of the "Great White Fleet," which was to take it 45,000 miles in fourteen months, had begun.

As the Panama Canal was far from finished, the ships made the long first leg of their voyage by way of Rio, the Strait of Magellan, and the west coast of South America. The fleet's first foreign port was Port of Spain, Trinidad, where it was received with indifference, for the arrival of the Americans coincided with the opening of the horse-racing season. Their reception in Rio was much better. Officers and men alike had a good time. Perhaps the most noteworthy outcome of the occasion was the birth of the Shore Patrol. Evans was determined that his men, let loose in a glittering foreign capital, would be neither the cause nor the victims of trouble. The men did well by their admiral, and the city by the men. Even so, the Shore Patrol proved itself so effective that it has now become an institution, in evidence wherever a naval base is located or in whatever port a U.S. man-of-war may visit.

Buenos Aires also wished to entertain the Americans, but its ship channel was too shallow, and the fleet passed on. Not, however, before it had received a graceful salute, far at sea, from a squadron of neatly handled green-hulled Argentine cruisers. Farther south the fleet stopped at Punta Arenas on the Strait of Magellan, where the stores advertised special prices for the Americans. They were special, too. Twenty-five-dollar fox skins were available at forty, and seal, normally sold at fifty dollars, could be had for seventy-five.

The last part of the passage through the mountain-rimmed Magellan Strait was made through fog so thick that one could see neither the ship 400 yards ahead nor the one 400 yards astern—the interval that the battleships of the Great White Fleet normally maintained at all times. Eventually the last ship felt her bow rise on a broad Pacific swell, and all were safe once more.

Now the white column steamed north and at Valparaíso Bay saluted the President of Chile. Less than twenty years earlier Evans, in a gunboat, had been involved in that very same bay in an unpleasantness which nearly caused war between Chile and the United States. Two U.S. Navy men had been killed in a riot arising from a barroom brawl, and it was largely Evans' tact which prevented a major incident. But cordiality was the order now—as it was at Callao, the seaport to the Peruvian capital, Lima, where the fleet was entertained by bullfights. It continued north to Magdalena Bay, Mexico. There, by arrangement with the Mexican government, the Americans were able to spend a month at target practice, drill, and sports. Then they went on to California, where Admiral Evans, painfully ill with rheumatism, gave up his command.

After the men were banqueted at every port from San Diego to Seattle, Evans' replacement, Rear Admiral Charles S. Sperry, took the fleet to sea again, heading out across the Pacific in the beginning of July. The first stop was Honolulu. Chief turret captain Roman J. Miller of the *Vermont*, visiting nearby Pearl Harbor, found that though it was yet undeveloped, it was "from a naval point of view, a very important place." Leaving the Hawaiian Islands, the ships proceeded on a leisurely roundabout voyage, with stops at New Zealand, Australia, the Philippines, and Japan.

The Japanese, who only a short time before had been threatening war, received their white-hulled visitors with "cordiality . . . amounting often to actual frenzy," as one participant remembered. The Americans did more than enjoy the cordiality. Observing the Japanese fleet in dark war paint, many officers recommended that our ships also be painted for war at all times. To leave the ships white until strained relations occurred with another country and then to change their color would be, as one naval officer has pointed out, "an overt act that might precipitate the very enemy action that the diplomats might otherwise be able to forestall." The recomended change was put into effect within a few months, and our ships have worn gray in one shade or another ever since.

After Japan, the fleet was temporarily split—for target practice off Manila and on the China coast. Then, entering the Indian Ocean, the ships steamed for home. The long passage was broken only by a visit to Ceylon; there the American sailors from the farms of Kansas and Georgia caught glimpses of native villages hidden away in groves, far up in the mountains, and tea or rubber plantations. When the fleet arrived at Suez, in January, 1909, word came of an earthquake at Messina, in Sicily, which had killed 60,000 people. Help was desperately needed. One ship from the fleet was loaded with medical supplies and rushed ahead. Arriving ten days after the disaster, the rescue crews could do little but search for bodies.

On February 22, 1909—Washington's Birthday—the Great White Fleet steamed home at last, to be welcomed at Hampton Roads by T. R. in the presidential yacht *Mayflower*. The occasion marked his last significant accomplishment as Chief Executive; ten days later, he left the White House for good. It was an impressive end to a notable presidential career; in his autobiography Roosevelt could write with justifiable pride that the voyage of the Great White Fleet was "the most important service I rendered peace." As he said in a speech to Admiral Sperry and his men:

You have falsified every prediction of the prophets of failure. In all your long cruise not an accident worthy of mention has happened. . . . As a war machine, the fleet comes back in better shape than it went out. In addition, you, the officers and men of this formidable fighting force, have shown

yourselves the best of all possible ambassadors and heralds of peace. . . . We welcome you home to the country whose good repute among nations has been raised by what you have done.

The accomplishments of the Great White Fleet had been numerous indeed. In his report for 1909 the Secretary of the Navy stated that the cruise "increased enlistments and enabled the Bureau of Navigation to recruit the enlisted force to practically its full strength," a pleasing development in a period when few American boys thought seriously of joining the Navy. Moreover, the Secretary was able to report, "There has been a gratifying decrease in the percentage of desertions, which has dropped from 9 to 5½ per cent during the past year."

The officers and men learned a great deal, too. They learned how to get the greatest economy out of their engines, the most mileage per ton of coal. Because they had no navy yards handy, they learned that to a great degree they could maintain their ships themselves. They learned to place their ships accurately on station during tactical drills and battle exercises, and to keep them there. At Magdalena Bay, early in the cruise, Admiral Evans said to one of his captains, "I hope your officers have learned something . . ." The captain replied, "Thirteen thousand miles at four hundred yards, night and day, including the Strait of Magellan; yes, they have learned a lot!"

More important, the cruise of the Great White Fleet demonstrated beyond question that the United States was now a world power. Those battleships, as they dipped their curved beaks into the rollers of the Pacific, the calm stretches of the Indian Ocean, and the white-flecked Mediterranean, were dramatic evidence of the radical change of course which this country, however unwitting and unwilling, had now taken.

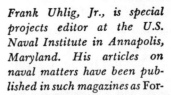

Frank Uhlig, Jr., is special projects editor at the U.S. Naval Institute in Annapolis, Maryland. His articles on naval matters have been published in such magazines as Foreign Affairs *and the* U.S. Naval Institute Proceedings.

For further reading: The Influence of Seapower Upon History, *by Alfred Thayer Mahan (Hill and Wang, 1957);* Admirals of the American Empire, *by Richard S. West, Jr. (Bobbs-Merrill, 1948); and* From Midshipman to Rear Admiral, *by Bradley A. Fiske (Century, 1919).*

Voyage Pittoresque aux Etats Unis de l'Amérique

CONTINUED FROM PAGE 51

and the people had proved themselves worthy of their dearly won liberties. Because of lack of experience the army was in poor shape, but the individual soldiers were brave, and given adequate training they would excel the armies of other countries. The multiplicity of races and religious sects gave strange and wonderful testimony to a spirit of true tolerance and of humanitarianism, a spirit Svinin noted elsewhere in the numerous and well-managed charitable institutions and the notably progressive penal institutions. Thanks to the broadening influence of popular education, every American *muzhik* could intelligently discuss an astonishing range of topics. And so on.

As in Freneau's time, an influential part of the American press was again beating the drums against the Russian menace. While Svinin was still here, the War of 1812 broke out. As we struggled with England, Russia—allied with our enemy and others—swept into France, banished Napoleon to Elba, and won new importance in the European balance of power.

Thomas Jefferson's friend Czar Alexander, who earlier had offered to negotiate a just peace in our own war, had rather given support to our adversary, and his barbarians had covered themselves with French watches as booty from a more civilized world (in much the same way, Soviet troops would collect wristwatches during World War II). To Hezekiah Niles, editor of the influential *Niles Weekly Register,* the worst was only too true. Catherine, he reminded his readers, had murdered her husband and afterward lived in "open whoredom" with "a regiment of male prostitutes"; Alexander was a parricide; and the Cossacks were bloodthirsty savages "but little milder than some of the Indians of North America." "God help the world," wailed the editor, "when *religion, order,* and *law* are to be supported by Russians." In keeping with this sorry estimate of the Russian character, the Russian consul general was arrested and briefly jailed in Philadelphia the following year on a charge of having raped a twelve-year-old servant girl.

However ineffective his reports on Russia were in America, Svinin's reports on the United States seem to have fared well enough abroad. His *Picturesque Voyage in North America,* published in St. Petersburg in 1815, went into a second edition within a few years and was promptly translated into Dutch and German. As the first eyewitness reports by an intelligent and perceptive Russian, his writings must have been read with particular interest by his liberal-minded countrymen. In 1818 Svinin established the review *Otechesteenniya Zapiski,* to which he occasionally contributed articles on American history and affairs until the publication folded in 1830. In all events, the romantic admiration for America that helped to fire the most enlightened Russian revolutionaries did not diminish after Svinin's return to his homeland. One of the most prominent and radical of them, who was shortly afterward hanged for conspiracy against the czarist regime, wrote an opinion which history has underscored with irony: "There are no good governments but in America."

Across the Atlantic, the old specter of a Russian invasion gradually faded from public memory, to be replaced by a different and completely contrary image, and one that had no more real substance. For generations of Americans, Catherine came to be remembered not as that "ravenous she-bear" whose hordes once threatened our shores, but rather as the "mother" of our independence who had refused her troops to George III and whose policy of armed neutrality had done so much at a critical period of the American Revolution to distract England's sea power. On both counts, of course, Catherine's unselfish interest in our cause was vastly overrated. As well she might, she had been playing her own game.

Nevertheless, during the waning months of World War I, American liberals chose to remember her refusal to provide an invasion force and on this score protested the use of American doughboys in Siberia and North Russia to aid in suppressing the Bolshevists. But international relationships at the level of state diplomacy are not and never have been directed by sentimental motives. Over the course of a century and a half, until quite recent years, Russia (like continental China) remained one of the most constant, traditional friends of the United States because there was no actual conflict of national interest. What would have been the difference in history, one wonders, if hireling Cossacks had come to America instead of the substitute Hessians? Conversely, one wonders how different the course of more recent American-Russian relations might have been had the two nations always exchanged envoys with the open mind and superb powers of observation that characterized young Paul Svinin.

Marshall B. Davidson, formerly director of publications for the Metropolitan Museum of Art, is the author of Life in America, *a social and cultural history of the United States. He has recently been appointed editor of* HORIZON *Magazine.*

For further reading: America Faces Russia, *by Thomas A. Bailey (Cornell University, 1950);* The American Impact on Russia, 1784–1917, *by Max M. Laserson (Collier, 1962).*

READING, WRITING, AND HISTORY

By BRUCE CATTON

Portraits of a President

The picture any President presents to the public is unlikely to be the picture he himself sees. It may not even be the picture seen by those who are closest to him. Neither the camera nor the typewriter is apt to make a wholly accurate portrayal—partly, no doubt, because the White House is inevitably a distorting glass whose images are always subject to a certain amount of retouching, and partly too because any human being, whether he be President of the United States or the humblest voter in a remote precinct, is always a good deal more complex than is commonly realized.

Anyway, it is hard to feel sure that we are seeing any President as he really was, and the amount of exposure a President gets does not help very much. By design or by accident, an image is created, usually fairly early in the game, and what comes later tends to conform to it. We ourselves, as spectators, even help make it conform; we have our own notion of the man, and we are likely to cling to it, discarding bits of evidence that do not fit our preconceived pattern.

There is available now a remarkable collection of pictures of one of the best-known of all American Presidents, Abraham Lincoln: *Lincoln in Photographs,* compiled by Charles Hamilton and Lloyd Ostendorf and containing, as far as the authors are able to determine—and they have spent years in careful search—every existing photograph of the man. In all, 119 separate photographs of Lincoln are reproduced here; good

pictures and poor ones, pictures wholly familiar and pictures nobody but specialists ever saw before, the sum total actually providing something of a new look at the man. It is of course possible that other pictures do exist somewhere, and from time to time one or another of them may come to light, but at the moment this is the most complete collection there is, and succeeding years are not likely to add much to it.

It goes without saying that the book is wholly fascinating, and it contains a few minor surprises.

It is a little surprising, for instance, to see how many photographs of Lincoln there actually are. The camera was a fairly new device when he was in the White House, and it was cumbersome. There was no corps of White House news photographers because news photographers in the modern sense did not exist. No man could take a snapshot then; every picture was a time exposure, and most pictures were taken in the studio, carefully posed and lighted. Today a President can hardly put his head out of the front door without being photographed, but it was very different in the 1860's. Indeed, one of the minor surprises here is the comparatively large number of pictures made out of doors, some of them entirely unposed.

Most of the pictures, of course, are studio shots, and some of the less familiar of these are extremely interesting. The best of them tend to come before Lincoln got into the White House; the public image had not been wholly developed, and there was less compulsion on the photographer's part to make the man look like what he was supposed to look like. There is, for example, a photograph made apparently in Decatur,

Illinois, in the spring of 1860, showing a clean-shaven man looking into the camera, and this picture does not give us the legendary Lincoln. This one shows a very hard man indeed, a man who could be ruthless and tough, using other men and then discarding them once they had served his purpose. The "real" Lincoln? Well, part of him: the trouble is there were so many real Lincolns that it is hard to pin one down.

Now and then the retouchers got to work, with disastrous results. One virtue of this book is that here and there it shows an original photograph alongside the retouched version, proving clearly that the Madison Avenue gambit was known in the sixties even though Madison Avenue then had not really been invented.

The earlier pictures, in short, tend to show a man who came up the hard way, a veteran of Illinois politics and of prairie life who carried on his face the relief map printed by what he had been, done, and lived through. It becomes easy to understand the remark of a London newspaperman who looked at an 1860 picture and said that it showed "an honest old

---

Lincoln in Photographs: An Album of Every Known Pose, by Charles Hamilton and Lloyd Ostendorf. University of Oklahoma Press. 409 pp. $19.50.

---

lawyer, with a face half Roman, half Indian, wasted by climate, scarred by a life's struggle."

The biggest struggle, of course, lay ahead, and many of the pictures made after Lincoln got into the White House are oddly disappointing. The "hard lines in his face," mentioned by an old-time friend, tend to vanish; what we too often get is a picture that conforms to the legend of the brooding, kindly, love-everybody President. One reason for this is fairly simple: it took time to make a picture then, and the man who was being photographed had to hold a fixed expression, sometimes for as much as a minute. As a result, a man who was being photographed posed. He had to pose; there was no other way to do it; but the picture was apt to show the pose rather than the man.

Mrs. Lincoln, as the authors of this book point out, once remarked that when Lincoln went to the studio he put on his "photographer's face," not because he was trying to strike an attitude but simply because that was the way the camera worked then. So something essential is missing. We have no picture of Lincoln laughing, although laughter was a vital part of him; we have nothing that catches him unaware, and we think of him as one always melancholy, sad, with features set in a mold. An acquaintance called the turn on this: "His large bony face when in repose was unspeakably sad and as unreadable as that of a sphinx, his eyes were as expressionless as those of a dead fish;

but when he smiled or laughed at one of his own stories or that of another then everything about him changed; his figure became alert, a lightning change came over his countenance, his eyes scintillated and I thought he had the most expressive features I had ever seen on the face of a man."

That Lincoln the camera never caught, and we are the poorer for it. There are some pictures, however, which seem to have something a little different. There are a few full-length pictures, and some that show the man seated in a straight-backed chair, which give us a new view: a long, lanky man, muscular, craggy of features, with long legs, knobby knees, and big feet, a man who down within was as hard as all the rocks in the western mountains, tenaciously pulling the nation along to victory in spite of all the odds.

Yet by and large one finishes an inspection of these pictures—as one finishes his study of almost everything the man's contemporaries wrote about him—wishing that one knew what Lincoln really looked like. The legend wins. We have this simulacrum of Lincoln, built up by the writings of worshipful men, sustained by innumerable photographs of the kindly, sad, warmhearted President, and we look at and for someone who was not always there. Where is the Lincoln we do not really know? Here and there, in this wonderful collection, there is a hint, but it is never much more than a hint. Perhaps the Presidency itself puts a veil over a man. Perhaps we never can be sure that we understand the man in the White House.

By the President Himself

Indeed, the exact picture may lie forever out of our reach. Even the searching portrayal of television can hardly remove the veil; perhaps the Presidency must always hide the man. No President was ever subjected to such intense, intimate, friendly portrayal as John F. Kennedy received during the weekend following his assassination—and yet in the end we really know just about what we had known before. We did come to learn a good deal about ourselves, and the knowledge undoubtedly was good for us, but our picture of Mr. Kennedy remains just what it always was, ennobled by the memory of solemn ceremonies, flag-draped casket, and immense silent crowds, but still essentially unchanged. Perhaps any man who lives in the White House inevitably steps just a little out of clear focus.

Even the man who has himself been a President cannot always paint a clear portrait. A man who survives his time in the White House and sits down in the pleasant twilight of life to tell what he did and what he meant can fail just as the cameras of Mathew Brady and Alexander Gardner failed.

One man who lived in the White House in time of immense crisis was General Dwight D. Eisenhower, who won in the hearts of the people a place almost as warm and abiding as Lincoln's. Now General Eisenhower has given us his own portrayal of his career as President, and his new book, *Mandate for Change*, is oddly similar to this book of Lincoln pictures: interesting, heart-warming, and somewhat baffling.

Undertaking to tell us all, General Eisenhower actually tells us very little. He describes, to be sure, the acts he did in order to get into the White House, and he goes into detail on the acts done after he got there, and to the best of his ability, presumably, he tells us what was on his mind when he did these things and how it all looks to him now that he is the squire of sunny acres at Gettysburg. Yet something is missing. It is as if General Eisenhower did what Mrs. Lincoln said that earlier President did: he put on his photographer's face when he got into the studio. Out of it we get an excellent picture of a man deservedly admired and revered, but we retain the haunting feeling that somewhere, somehow, an essential part of the picture got left out.

Here was a man, clearly, who knew how to be tough, a man used to command who could be ruthless, a leader who hewed to a chosen line so tenaciously that the country found itself following without quite understanding what had happened to it. Taking office as the leader of the political opposition, he managed to conserve most of the important things built by the men he had opposed—which is to say that he clung to collective security, NATO, the Marshall Plan, the concept of the United Nations as a force for peace, the broad idea of firmness in defense of America's vital interests which could still go hand in hand with a determination to keep the world from erupting into a new war. He took the country with him on these matters, and

Mandate for Change, 1953–1956, by Dwight D. Eisenhower. Doubleday & Company. 650 pp. $6.95.

the danger that a resurgence of old-time isolationism might cause us to repeat the mistakes of the 1920's was averted. Obviously, it took a good man to do this, and it took some struggles.

Yet as we read about all of this we get the odd feeling that the General was nothing more than a friendly, kindly man who simply followed his country's conscience without kicking anyone in the shins or stirring up any particular antagonisms. Obviously, this picture is as misleading as the comparable picture of the gentle, compassionate, always kindly Lincoln.

As President, he exercised the virtue of restraint. Given the circumstances under which he took office, this was wise and proper. But now, with office behind him, with no obligation upon him except to speak his own mind, the virtue of restraint is still dominant. General Eisenhower rarely lets us see the man who held the presidential office. In speaking of the Quemoy-Matsu problem, during which his administration met and passed a test which might easily have led to an all-out war, he remarks: "The hard way is to have the courage to be patient." True enough: but it would be interesting now to know just whom he had to be most patient with, and what he thought about the people involved, and how he sustained himself in his exercise of patience. This sort of thing we do not get.

Any man, obviously, whether he is a former President or a man who once served as county commissioner, is entitled to write his memoirs in his own way, and it is hardly fair to quarrel with him for the things he refuses to say. But *Mandate for Change* remains singularly like *Lincoln in Photographs*. It tells us some things we did not know, casts a bit of light here and there on matters not previously illuminated, and presents a series of fascinating first-hand portraits; yet somehow it leaves us with the feeling that we still do not quite have the full picture. The live, passionate, interesting man who was President during those fateful years remains behind a mist of vague generalities and happy expressions of good feeling for almost everybody.

Concluding his summary of the achievements of his first term, General Eisenhower writes:

"We had converted the United States of America from a nation at war to a nation at peace, productive and happy. We had wrought the giant military structures which, coiled for war, would safeguard that peace. We had ringed the globe by signed agreements with our allies. And hour by hour we had made clear to friend and foe our determination to safeguard freedom in those areas where freedom was prized, and we had given hope for a better life to many millions who, unless backed by our strength, would almost certainly lose the freedom and economic opportunities that they now could devote their full energies to achieve."

That statement, which fairly well stands the test of comparison with the record, is a statement of genuine achievement not easily gained. But it cannot all have been done in an atmosphere of sweetness, light, and good-fellowship. Telling about it, the General somehow donned his photographer's face. We miss the sense of strain, struggle, and devotion that undoubtedly lay back of the achievement.

It really is hard to get a truly realistic portrait of a President.

110

ALBERT B. COREY
1898—1963

CHARLES GOTTLIEB

Albert B. Corey was a gifted historian who believed that true history is of the people, by the people, and for the people.

As he saw it, history is basically the record of things done by ordinary, everyday folk who try to earn a living, to get a little fun out of life, and to serve their ideals and fellow men as best they can. They contribute the faith and quiet courage which make possible the bright deeds of their famous leaders; out of what they want and do and believe in come the great, seemingly impersonal forces and movements that make up the formal story of historic events. They not only make history: they are ultimately the ones to whom history's story has to be directed.

Dr. Corey was State Historian of New York; as someone aptly remarked, he was thus a sort of "family historian" to millions of citizens who wanted to know more about their immediate backgrounds. He was also, from 1950 to 1954, president of the American Association for State and Local History, which gave him a broader field in which to perform the same function. He was intensely interested in the quarterly publication which the Association had begun in 1949— a modest but distinctive little magazine called *American Heritage,* which tried to tell people about their past in terms of the homely, familiar deeds and events that lie at the bottom of all human achievement.

During the latter part of his term as Association president Dr. Corey realized that the publication needed a firmer base and a larger audience. The Association could no longer carry it, because it could not reach very far beyond its own membership. The little magazine must either get new resources or go out of existence.

Dr. Corey wanted it to live and grow. He believed that it could do this as a commercial enterprise, because he believed that the general public would support it in such a way that it could realize its full potential. When it was proposed, early in 1954, that ownership of the magazine be transferred to a new publishing corporation that would put this matter to the test, he welcomed the proposal and supported it vigorously.

As a result, the American Heritage Publishing Company came into being, and AMERICAN HERITAGE Magazine was transformed into the publication that now exists. Its experience has shown that Dr. Corey's confidence was justified. During the difficult period of transition from a small, specialized magazine to one that reaches a large audience, Dr. Corey's wise advice, counsel, and assistance were invaluable.

If it had not been for Albert B. Corey, this magazine today would not exist. His untimely death on November 9, 1963, from an automobile accident robbed us of a valued counsellor and an even more deeply valued friend. These lines are written in tribute to a man to whom we are profoundly indebted.

—Bruce Catton

HOW A LADY ANSWERS A LETTER

The Approach Timorous

Miss Henderson:

I beg to apologize for addressing you thus, being an entire stranger; but having the misfortune to be unknown to you is my excuse for this strange proceeding, which, I am well aware, is entirely at variance with the rules of etiquette. I have for two sabbaths seen you at church, and I am frank to confess that your appearance has made so deep an impression upon me as to make me extremely desirous of forming your acquaintance. I am, at present, a clerk in the ribbon department at Smith & Brown's store. Will you do me the great favor of allowing this to commence a friendship, which, I trust, will never be regretted by yourself. Please deign to give me at least a single line in reply to this, and oblige,

Your Sincere Admirer,
Wesley Barnum.

The Freeze Deep

Mr. Barnum.

Dear Sir:

I considerably question whether it is due to propriety to answer your note at all. But as you might fear that your letter had miscarried, and thus be induced to write again, it is best, probably, for me to make an immediate reply, and thus settle the affair entirely, and relieve you, possibly, of further suspense. It will be impossible for me to recognize you, or to think under any circumstances of permitting an acquaintance to be commenced by such an introduction as you seem to deem sufficient. More especially should I regret allowing a friendship to be formed by recognitions in the hours of divine service in church, while the mind should be employed in religious observances. You will, therefore, please understand that I am not favorable to further recognition, nor to a continuance of correspondence.

Amelia Henderson.

The Thaw, Slight

Mr. Barnum.

Dear Sir:

I am in receipt of your note, and must confess that I am surprised at your request. I am entirely opposed to commencing, on general principles, an acquaintance with such an introduction, and consider it very improper, especially to allow it to originate in church during the hours of divine service. Were it not that I think your meaning kind and your intentions good, I would return your letter unanswered. As it is, I will take your request under consideration, and, if I think best to grant it, you may know of the fact by my recognition at the close of the service in the Sabbath School.

Respectfully,
Amelia Henderson.

FROM AN ENTIRE STRANGER

These sample letters come from Hill's Manual of Social and Business Forms, a cold-hearted how-to-do-it book first published in 1873. General Grant and the governor of Massachusetts publicly endorsed it. Somehow romance survived.